If you read this
and want to pass it on to
write a note and write.

You can also post about it in the
Facebook.com/ScarsToStarsLive group.

To Sam,

Thank you for your support, kindness and friendship. Keep on thriving!

:)

Erik
x

ADVANCE PRAISE

"Whether you are looking for inspiration and the feeling that you are not alone on one of your darkest days, or insight and understanding about a life challenge that you have not personally experienced but wish you knew how to support, *Scars to Stars* brings you on an intimate journey with authors who bravely share their trials and tribulations and how they turned them into a positive outlook. As a therapist I need stories like this to help motivate my clients and myself. I love the format of short powerful chapters which each give me something unexpected and thought provoking and that end with a much needed scoop of hope on top. In particular, Erik DaRosa's story of transforming his life from a man who was trapped in a prison of anxiety and shame about his mental health challenges to an advocate for breaking the stigma and sharing our journeys is a story I think so many men can relate to and need to hear. I cannot imagine any person who would not benefit from, and genuinely enjoy, reading this book."

—DANIEL MAIGLER, LCSW
Mental Health Advisor, Paws for Patrick
Host of Not Allowed to Die Podcast, Life Enthusiast

"*Scars to Stars* was a very deep read. It touched my soul reading some of the stories and was very emotional but motivational as well. This book is a great testament to God's greatness and his healing powers."

—IMANI DIXON, Professional Basketball Player

"*Scars to Stars, vol 3,* is an inspiring and moving book full of stories of overcoming conflict and hardships. This book will help anyone who is struggling and looking for the light of Jesus Christ."

—VICTORINE E. LIESKE, New York Times Bestselling Author

"These stories shared in *Scars to Stars* are deeply personal and empowering, offering intimate glimpses of our human condition. Individually and collectively, these glimpses are all about healing, wholeness, and self-discovery. They are about turning vulnerability into strength, and the courage required to face the darkness and make it conscious, for the sake of finding our true light."

—WAYNE ALLEN LeVINE

"*Scars to Stars* is a beautiful tribute to the tenacity of human spirit enveloping opportunities to open deep and festering wounds to create change. Each human being included in the *Scars to Stars* compilation has a poignant and bittersweet story to share as they bravely come forward, one by one. Each reveal in some way that we are not alone in our pain. The riveting authentic retelling of trauma and scarring lead to profound integration, with compassion and dignity as a human collective and each story told melds into the background. While the compilation is mostly female, there are a few from the male point of view including Erik DaRosa, who describes what it feels like when we break the cycle of silence by sharing our mental health struggles for the first time. His first dissociative episode in 2004 led him to reach out for help, and learn why it's important that we not struggle in silence. Each story is told with grace and aplomb. There are no whining victims here. Luckily for the reader. we may be the fly on the wall gaining understanding, compassion, and connection for our human trajectory as one. A must read, a must savor, a must pass-it-along compilation of hope, understanding and authentic inspiration.

—SUSAN GOLD, Montana

"I didn't know how much I needed this. When I stumbled upon this book, I realized down to the very people that were involved, it was similar to my story. I knew I had to read this book. Everyone in the book was so brave and inspirational."

—KAY, Amazon review

SCARS
— to —
STARS

VOLUME 3

STORIES OF VULNERABILITY, RESILIENCE,
AND OVERCOMING ADVERSITY

AMAZON BESTSELLING SERIES
Foreword by Deana Brown Mitchell

Copyright © 2023 The Realize Foundation

All Rights Reserved

Year of the Book
135 Glen Avenue
Glen Rock, PA 17327

Print ISBN: 978-1-64649-336-4
Ebook ISBN: 978-1-64649-337-1

This book or parts thereof may not be reproduced in any form, stored in any retrieval system, or transmitted in any form by any means—electronic, mechanical, photocopy, recording, or otherwise—without prior written permission of the publisher, except as provided by United States of America copyright law.

Scripture taken from the New King James Version®. Copyright © 1982 by Thomas Nelson. Used by permission. All rights reserved.

CONTENTS

Foreword *by Deana Brown Mitchell* 1

From Touched to Empowered *by Katie Miller* 5

Victim to Victor *by Keith Hanks* 19

The Story You Try Hardest Not to Tell *by Lori Ann Hood* 31

Beauty for Ashes *by Karyn Harper* 39

Tell Someone *by Erik DaRosa* 51

Feeling the Fear and Doing it Anyway *by Corrine Thomas* 65

Blessings Within a Moment *by Deb Weilnau* 73

"I Ain't Goin' Nowhere!" *by Marcia Dixon* 85

The End... But at What Cost? *by Patience Behymer* 97

"Show Me, Right Now!" *by Amy Charbonneau* 107

My Xcellence Matters *by Rev. Linda A. Housden, R.N.* 117

My Blurred Opinion *by Timothy "T.J." West* 131

A Tale of Two Cousins *by Chad Gaines* 141

Set Apart *by Ted McConnell* 149

From the Crack House to the White House *by Dr. Jacquala Shropshire* 157

Love is the Greatest Gift in Life *by Geoff Hudson-Searle* 165

Overcoming *by Devan Liam Featherstone* 179

Conclusion *by Deana Brown Mitchell* 187

Foreword

Deana Brown Mitchell

SOBBING SO UNCONTROLLABLY I COULD NOT TAKE A BREATH, heavily intoxicated but the pain was unbearable, washing down pills with an open bottle of wine that I grabbed from the fridge... I just wanted it all to stop... the pain... the fighting... the lies...

Waking up in the hospital to realize I was still alive was the ultimate feeling of failure.

Then the silence for 23 years until a dear friend succeeded in what I couldn't.

My pain that I hid for so many years came crashing back. I kept it at bay because I was so busy running an award-winning multimillion-dollar business. But then COVID-19 shut down everything including my business, my purpose, and my sanity.

Now what? I had no clients to keep me busy and I was alone with my thoughts, not sure what to do. I had to focus on something outside of myself or I would not be okay. I felt empty like I had nothing left to contribute to the world. I needed someone to depend on me to show up for something... I needed purpose.

This was the first time in my life there was no motivation... no promotion or achievement to strive for... no contracts to get signed... no clients holding me accountable. Work and striving for the next thing had always been my coping mechanism and now that was taken away in a day... March 13, 2020.

The months that followed were spent processing my journey of mental health and exploring new coping skills. God was calling me to a new purpose—helping other humans to realize they are not alone. The epiphany that conversations and community can save lives became my new obsession.

Scars to Stars™ was born to bring to life this new mission. It started as a virtual summit, then a three-day event and another summit. This new community is made up of incredible people who have been on similar journeys of overcoming, and now selflessly lend a hand or an ear, along with encouragement to others who need to understand they are not alone.

In these pages you will hear from:

KATIE MILLER, who teaches how you can help make teen suicide a thing of the past...

KEITH HANKS, who's turning the tide on PTSD and suicide in the first responder community...

LORI ANN HOOD, who counsels that the story you try hardest not to tell can be the biggest blessing for someone else ...

KARYN HARPER, whose victory over addiction and physical abuse shows that there is always hope for a brighter future...

ERIK DaROSA, whose journey finally changed for the better the moment he told someone...

CORRINE STATIA THOMAS, who shares how it's possible to feel the fear and do it anyway...

DEB WEILNAU, who has learned to recognize the beautiful blessings that were disguised as difficulties in the jigsaw puzzle of her life...

MARCIA DIXON, who conquered cancer with an "I ain't goin' nowhere" attitude ...

PATIENCE BEHYMER, who grew up burdened by the fear of a mother who struggled with emotional pain to the point of life and death...

AMY CHARBONNEAU, whose desperate prayer for the evidence of God's love came in the form of her sleepy-eyed toddler...

REV. LINDA A. HOUSDEN, R.N., who was 17 when she first invited Jesus into her heart, but now at 71 is still learning to accept a deeper consciousness of God...

TIMOTHY "T. J." WEST, who as a child lost his vision but has not lost his will to live and help others conquer disabilities...

CHAD GAINES, who survived emotional and physical abuse, only to witness his mother kill his stepdad...

TED McCONNELL, who found love and acceptance in a foster family...

JACQUALA SHROPSHIRE, Ph.D., whose only thought was once finding the next high, who now devotes her life to serving others...

GEOFF HUDSON-SEARLE, who shares that we can all do amazing things when we focus our passion...

DEVAN LIAM FEATHERSTONE, who survived personal trauma and seemingly lost everything, as he journeys to find justice and follow his destiny...

We are all like diamonds in the night sky... all shapes and sizes. We are individuals formed under pressure. We are one of a kind with unique talents, skills, and character.

The authentic, vulnerable stories in these pages may be similar to yours or may be so different that they are unfathomable. My hope is that they encourage, inspire, and motivate you to explore your own journey in this life to find your true purpose and happiness.

You matter... you are worthy... and you are enough.

FIND OUT MORE

- ➤ **Scars to Stars™**
  - Buy the Book, Gift the Book, Donate the Book
    - Amazon, Barnes & Noble Website, Walmart Website
  - **Join the Scars to Stars LIVE Facebook Group**
    - https://www.facebook.com/groups/scarstostarslive
  - **Listen to the Scars to Stars Podcast**
    - https://feeds.captivate.fm/scars-to-stars-podcast/
  - **Visit our YouTube channel**
    - https://www.youtube.com/@realizefoundation5598

- ➤ **The Realize Foundation** https://realizefoundation.org/
  - Learn more about our **mission**
  - Take the FREE **H.O.P.E. Course**
  - **DONATE** to our cause
  - **Tell Your Story** (application on website, Scars to Stars page, QR Code Below)

- ➤ **Announcing our brand-new MEMBERSHIP!**
  - Learn more by scanning the QR Code Below

Membership   *Tell Your Story*

FROM TOUCHED TO EMPOWERED

KATIE MILLER

IN THE MID-TO-LATE 1990s, I WAS IN HIGH SCHOOL. Most middle class families did not own a cellphone during this time.

"Katie, phone!"

I heard my mom call from the kitchen. I ran up the stairs from my room, wondering which friend had phoned. Thoughts ran through my head about possible get-togethers, sleep-overs, or trips to the mall. When I got to the kitchen, I picked the phone receiver up from the table and gasped, *"Hello?"*

I heard a whispered, *"Katie... I need help."*

"Sure, what's up?" I responded, thinking my friend needed help with a homework assignment or something. What I heard caused my stomach to drop to the floor.

"I made a mistake. I swallowed a handful of my mom's muscle relaxers. I'm having a hard time staying awake."

Even now, more than twenty-five years later, I do not recall the rest of the conversation with my friend. What I do recall was the panic I felt because I did not have her mother's work phone number.

I remember my friend dropping the phone and not responding.

I remember the panic in my voice when speaking to the 911 operator and realizing I did not even know my friend's home address.

What I do recall is calling my friend back and being happy the phone was answered, acknowledging that 911 was on the other line. I remember hanging up and asking my mom to drive me to my friend's house. But Mom refused, stating we did not want to be in the way when the ambulance arrived.

I don't recall how much time passed as I worried and fumed at my mother for not letting me be at my friend's side. I do remember getting a call from my friend's mom.

"Katie, what happened?" I vaguely remember providing the details my friend gave me over the phone and explained about me calling 911. The next question is one I will never forget. *"How could you let this happen?"*

A sense of dread washed over me. I whispered, *"What do you mean?"*

Whatever else was said, the only thing I remember is a sense of guilt and shame. How could I have not seen my friend was struggling? Why did I not tell someone what things I did notice,

> *I heard a whispered, "Katie... I need help!"*

yet were completely irrelevant? What could I have shared that would not have broken the trust of our friendship?

I remember returning to school, and my friend being distant. We did eventually speak, and I found out that she had her stomach pumped. We drifted apart after that and were no longer best friends. By high school graduation, we barely spoke to each other.

The two of us reconnected a few years later, hung out for a bit, then lost touch again. This happened several times until the mid to late 2000s. The last conversation I recall was asking my friend's opinion about a job opportunity on the other side of the U.S. The conversation felt awkward, but I don't recall why. We drifted apart again.

In August 2019, my sister Stephanie gave a 7-minute talk about her first suicide attempt at the age of 13 and the multiple attempts that followed over the years. I was not there when she gave this talk, but heard about it after the fact. What shocked me was that I remember more details around the event involving my friend than my sister.

The shame and guilt from that one question my friend's mother asked me came back with full force when I couldn't recall details of my sister's multiple attempts. Stephanie shared that she still has suicidal thoughts, but finds the joy of living every day, and wants to share those tools with teens before they need them.

This was the launch of the Teen Suicide Prevention Society in April 2020, just before schools were closed due to COVID and the suicide rate over all demographics shot through the roof.[1]

> *The only thing I remember is a sense of guilt and shame.*

Since the formation of the Teen Suicide Prevention Society, or TSPS for short, we studied how the teenage brain really works and how to break open the echo chamber of negative thoughts.

When asked why they attempted, we learned that most suicide attempt survivors would respond with "I don't know." We also learned that the prefrontal cortex starts developing during adolescence, but is not fully formed until approximately age 25. This is the part of the brain is designed for personality expression, decision-making, planning complex cognitive behavior, and moderating social behavior.

This is why we created a script, a practice guide, to use when having the "Talk That Saves Lives." It is created with neutral language, and is designed to "practice" with a partner. When you get the guide, you will see we include the invitation to have a practice conversation. This way the person you are asking does not feel judged. You share the rules of the conversation: "You can only say Yes or No for the first three questions. Then on the fourth question, you can tell me as much as you want."

Because the other person has agreed to help you "practice" the Talk That Saves Lives, they are aware of the topic. This way they do not feel judged. And because you shared these rules with them, they understand that the questions might be uncomfortable and that

---

[1] Per the National Alliance of Mental Illness website, suicide is the second leading cause of death among people aged 10–14 and the third leading cause of death among people aged 15-24 in the U.S.

only saying yes or no is allowed for the first three questions. This reduces any stress or anxiety that might pop up when the questions are asked.

The final question is: "What are your reasons for staying?" They can tell you as much as they want. You want them to tell you as many reasons as possible. By answering this question out loud, their brain adds a notation that these reasons are important and need to be saved. Their brain creates a file of their "reasons for staying."

Today, I realize the accusatory question my friend's mother asked all those years ago was just what popped out of her mouth in the moment. She was still trying to process what her child had done and why.

As a mother myself, I understand being in a situation when your teen does something you cannot understand. What I have learned is to take a deep breath before responding. This calms the heart rate, clears the mind, and allows me to take a moment to respond with love.

What are YOUR reasons for staying?

After all, I have no idea what is going on in my teenager's head. What I do know is that they are mine, I love them, and I would not change anything about them for the world.

And yes, I am using neutral language when it comes to my teenager. Why? *Because 45% of the youth who have serious thoughts of suicide are LGBTQ.*[2]

As a member of this community, it breaks my heart that nearly half of youth struggling with suicidal thoughts need one of the hardest conversations to have with their parents—claiming who they are, and who they love. And of the several hundred teenagers I have spoken with, the majority state the first response they heard from their parents was not a loving one.

---

[2] National Alliance on Mental Illness. (n.d.). Suicide Prevention Awareness Month. Retrieved from https://www.nami.org/Get-Involved/Awareness-Events/Suicide-Prevention-Awareness-Month.

So it has become part of my personal mission to discuss the importance of a "personal pause button" to stop the "knee-jerk" emotional response when something shocks us or catches us off guard.

In the book *The Dance of Connection: How to Talk to Someone When You're Mad, Hurt, Scared, Frustrated, Insulted, Betrayed, or Desperate*, author Harriet Lerner, a clinical psychologist, discusses the importance of feeling heard and understood in relationships. She argues that when we feel like we are not being heard, our emotions become overwhelming, and we may act out in unproductive ways. On the other hand, when we feel like we are being heard, our emotions are validated, and we are better able to work through them.

While this book doesn't provide a specific citation for the human need to be heard, it does provide an in-depth discussion of the importance of being heard in relationships and the negative consequences that can result when we feel like we are not being heard.

So I offer you the rules I now live by:
1. Speak your truth without fear.
2. Listen without judgment.
3. Respond with love.

I am including a copy of The Talk That Saves Lives below. Please feel free to share it and practice it.

You can always reach me at www.KT4TSPS.com

The Guide to The Talk That Saves Lives

You need this guide because...

Suicides are on the rise around the world. Here in North America, we're experiencing a suicide epidemic. We believe that suicide is an EVERYBODY PROBLEM to solve.

We've found that there's one in every room.

In every room you walk into, in-person or online, there's at least one person grieving the loss of a loved one to suicide, and in every room there's at least one person struggling to stay alive.

Our mission at the Teen Suicide Prevention Society is to end teen suicide. We believe that busting the myths, exposing the challenges, exploring the options, and most importantly, sharing the preventions is the fastest path to accomplish our mission, and we need speed because we've learned:

"You can't tell by looking."

You can't tell by looking who's at risk, who's grieving, or who's struggling. You can't tell by looking who's happy or who's masking. You can't tell by looking who's coping and who's lying.

You can't tell by looking who's a little down or who's so "down" they've forgotten what "up" feels like. So, instead of "waiting for signs" (a.k.a. "looking for trouble"), we recommend a more proactive approach.

Take action before you think it's needed, before your friend or loved one is obviously struggling.

Taking a pure-prevention approach gives your friends and loved ones a buffer between themselves and an edge they may not even know they're near (a.k.a. "suicide-proofing" them).

Suicide is an EVERYBODY problem

We call it "emotional cage fighting."

We know that some of your friends, your family, and your peers are dying for you to invite them out of "The Cage" they're in. They're afraid to talk about how they're feeling except in the most damaging ways possible...

Did you know that teens call suicide "self-deleting"? That's right... "self-deleting"... as if it's not a big deal. No different than hitting the delete key on a keyboard or ending a video game.

However, ending this game, the one we call "Life" is a little different.

1. It's permanent.

2. When one person takes their own life, they massively impact a minimum of 20 people who care about them.

3. Worse, when one person takes their own life, they give tacit permission for everyone who knows them to do the same. This is why suicide is considered a contagious "dis-ease."

4. Finally, odds are, those who are closest will end up saying: *"We never saw it coming."*

"We never saw it coming." These are the saddest five words in the world. I never want you to hear them said about a friend or loved one. I never ever want you to say them about a friend or loved one. And I never, ever, ever want your friends or loved ones to say them about YOU.

I want you to know that I've got your back. I'm not going to send you to get them out of "The Cage" alone or unarmed.

All I need to know is, are you willing?

Are you willing to fight for the lives of your friends and loved ones?

Are you willing to get into "The Cage" with them and pull them out before it's too late to "suicide-proof" them?

Thank you. Ready?

The key to going into "The Cage" with confidence and coming out with your friends and loved ones, and all your parts and pieces intact, including your relationships, is to simply follow "The Guide."

That's right, you've got a guide to help you prevent suicide.

It all starts with "The Invitation."

"The Invitation" and "The Talk" are both precisely formulated to work with how our human brains really process details. Both are neuroscience based and designed using a reflection technology that activates the mirror neurons in the brain and builds an emotional buffer around both you and your friend or loved one.

The Guide was first introduced January 16, 2021, in the TEDx Talk, *Have 'The Talk' to Stop Teen Suicide* at TEDx TenayaPaseo in Las Vegas. Since then, The Guide, also known as "The Talk That Saves Lives" has been delivered on hundreds of stages to thousands of listeners, each a little more suicide-proofed after listening. But the real magic happens when you have "The Talk" one-on-one.

Let's get started. Please read the words out loud by yourself first and then practice with a family member or good friend. Be honest and direct. Speak your truth. Read directly from The Guide and you won't ever have to figure out what to say. We've done that for you.

The Invitation:

> Hi, I've joined the mission to end teen suicide. They gave me a guide. I need to practice. Would you have a few minutes to help me practice my guide? It'll only take about 5 minutes.

Wait for them to respond. It's great if they want to make a plan for a different time or day. The Talk is often best if it's pre-planned. When it's time, come out swinging. Start with laying down the rules.

The Talk:

> Thank you for agreeing to help me practice the guide to stop suicide. I'm going to be reading it to you so that I don't miss anything. There are only four questions and one rule.
>
> The rule: You can only answer "Yes" or "No" to the first three questions. Then on the fourth question, you can tell me as much as you want. Sound good?

Wait for them to agree before continuing.

> Thank you. Okay, here we go. Remember, you can only answer "Yes" or "No."
>
> Question 1: Have you heard about the rise in teen suicides?

Wait for them to respond before continuing. No matter what they say, you only respond by saying, "Thank you," and nothing else until after all the questions have been answered.

> Thank you. Question 2: Do you have a story? Do you have a friend who's tried or died?

Wait for them to respond before continuing. Remember, you only respond with, "Thank you," and nothing more, *no matter what they say and no matter if they remember the rule or not.* The questions are written in specific, trigger-neutral language. That's why you always read them from The Guide. It's important to NEVER "wing it" in an Emotional Cage Fight.

> Thank you. Question 3: Have you ever thought of leaving that way?

Wait for them to respond. Breathe. No matter what they say, respond only with, "Thank you."[3]

> Thank you. Question 4: Why stay? What are your reasons for staying?

Smile! Listen. Prompt. Keep them talking about their reasons for staying by prompting with:[4]

> "Tell me more," or "What else?"

---

[3] If your friend or loved one has thoughts of leaving, don't panic. Thoughts of leaving are normal. They're part of the natural negative bias, worst-case scenario, problem-solving mechanism in our brains. Thoughts of leaving are only a problem if they hang around and form what we call a "negative echo chamber."

[4] If your friend or loved one has "thoughts of leaving" and zero "reasons for staying," please stay with them and call "988" or your local suicide intervention hotline. If they refuse to talk to an intervention specialist at the hotline, stay with them and call "911" or your local police department's emergency number. Oh, they may hate you for it, and it'll be worth it if it helps them stay.

Smile even more. Listen. If they start to slow down, prompt for more with:

> "What's so good about your life that you want more of it?"

Smile more. Listen more. Resist sharing your own reasons for staying unless they ask you. This is their time and what you'll be witnessing will be amazing. When they're done, respond with:

> Thank you. I loved what you shared about (one of their reasons for staying.)

If they ask, you can share about the mission to end teen suicide. You can tell them about how to get their own Guide. You can help them find more reasons for staying. When you're finished, please share with them how we feel about you:

> Thank you for playing. Thank you for staying. And most importantly, thank you for being you and doing what you do. What you do is important and who you are is AMAZING!

DISCLAIMER: Out of thousands of talks, the number of times someone has had the combination of "thoughts of leaving" and zero "reasons for staying" is zero. Our brains are hardwired to answer questions. This means that the brain will come up with reasons for staying when you ask Question 4. It has to, because we're just wired that way, and every answer they give builds out a bigger buffer between them and an edge they may not have even known they were near.

Here's a quick overview of why "The Talk" works to build out that buffer to pull them out of "The Cage."

The first three questions activate and then agitate all the angst they have on the topic of suicide. The questions are closed-ended to keep your friends and loved ones from going into their painful stories. Once agitated, there's a lot of emotionally charged neural-electrical activity happening in the brain.

You only respond to their answers with "Thank you" to prevent you from probing and accidentally triggering or re-traumatizing them.

The minute you ask Question 4, their brain takes all of that emotionally charged neural-electricity and redirects it into the search for reasons for staying. What happens in their brains as soon as they start answering the question is nothing short of magical. With the first answer, their brain builds out a new neural pathway. Then, as you probe, and they keep coming up with additional reasons for staying, their brain builds out a whole neural network, a sort of mental file folder, labeled: "Reasons for Staying."

What's so good about this new neural network is that the filter in the brain known as the Reticular Activating System, or RAS, gets recalibrated so that now when a naturally occurring thought of leaving comes up, it bumps up against this new mental file folder, labeled "Reasons for Staying," and the thought of leaving is less likely to stay around.

We believe there's a second benefit of using this guide and having this talk. The second benefit comes from another brain-thing called "mirror neurons." Thanks to mirror neurons, when your friends and loved ones start sharing their reasons for staying, your brain starts matching up your own reasons for staying at the same time. This builds out a buffer between you and the edge as well. Truly a win-win.

We highly recommend having as many "Talks" as you can. Here's an easy way to know who to have a "Talk" with. Simply write down the names of all the people you would call to share about a new restaurant or to celebrate receiving a promotion or winning an award. Then call each one in turn and invite them to help you practice this guide.

The more you practice with your friends and loved ones, the more emotionally resilient your whole tribe will become.

There are more great things in store for you over at the website. To learn more about the mission and check out the resources, visit www.TeenSuicidePreventionSociety.com

Learning "The Talk" helps improve all your relationships.

A thought to ponder: We're actively seeking teachers, preachers, healers, and parents willing to build their own emotional intelligence and resilience and then take this guide and our other tools into groups and schools.

If you want to know more, please take the 4-hour course on building emotional intelligence and resilience. At the end of the course, you'll be coated with layers of "emotional teflon," and you'll be certified to lead "The Talk That Saves Lives." There's no obligation to lead a group or make a presentation. What we've found is that taking the class improves your ability to communicate in an emotionally intelligent way and that improves all your relationships.

Details are available on the "Programs" tab on the website, and 100% of proceeds are used to fulfill the mission to make teen suicide a thing of the past.

Thank you again for being you, caring enough to read this guide, and most of all thank you for staying.

We believe:

Heaven doesn't need another angel.
Heaven knows we need you here.

Copyright © Teen Suicide Prevention Society, Inc.
All rights reserved in perpetuity.

Katie Miller

KATIE MILLER believes we sometimes need a pause button in our lives, a chance to take a deep breath and see there are always options. When Katie learned she was going to be a mom in 2003, she decided her child could talk to her about anything without fear of judgment. What she did not know was that she was laying the foundation for her mission with that one decision.

In August 2019, when her sister broke the silence of her suicide attempts, Katie knew there was more she could do to help others, yet was not sure how. Then the world pivoted due to COVID-19 in 2020, and the universal cry for help could no longer be ignored. Katie decided now was the time to share what she had learned.

As a Mind-Body Healing and Trauma Resolution Guide, Katie ardently strives to guide others in locating their purpose and rewiring their "emotional remote control." This empowers us to ignite our positive emotional states at will, rather than succumbing to negative triggers.

In her role as Assistant Director/Co-Founder of the Teen Suicide Prevention Society, Katie and her family are resolute in their endeavor to render suicide intervention programs obsolete. Their mission is steadfast—to eradicate the need for such interventions and pave the way for a brighter future.

www.TeenSuicidePreventionSociety.com

Victim to Victor

Keith Hanks

I GREW UP IN NORTH-CENTRAL MASSACHUSETTS in a poor family of mixed heritage—Irish, English, French, Native American, and Scandinavian. I was a mutt, so to speak. With strong roots in the fire service and military in my family, a duty to serve, protect, and love my community and country was instilled in me from birth.

My childhood was spent watching uncles race off to fires, car accidents, and other emergencies. I spent most of my time either at the fire station or my grandmother's, conveniently located two houses away. The other firefighters were "uncles" and their wives, aunts, also stepping in as babysitters from time to time. I just thought it was normal behavior to know how to roll a fire hose, climb a ladder, and put on firefighting coats and boots.

To most, when I begin to tell the story of my life, people typically say, "Wow! That must have been so much fun." And it was.

But my childhood had another aspect, a very dark part that was handed down to me from the elders, in an unwanted way.

The physical, emotional, psychological, and sexual abuse I went through for years, starting at age six, included being raped several times by members of my own family.

This abuse and associated events left me scarred, angry, and with a skewed set of emotions going into my teenage and young adult years. At age 13, I had a suicide attempt involving pills and alcohol. My family was none the wiser. I was filled with an overwhelming sense of guilt, shame, fear, anger, and above all else confusion.

My teenage years leading up to high school left me with lower-than-normal self-esteem and almost zero confidence in anything I did. I felt unloved, unsupported, and alone, even when I was with the few friends that I did have.

I always knew I was going to be a firefighter like the rest of my family, and after being medically declined by the Marines, that's just what I did. Two days after my 18th birthday, in the beginning of December of my senior year of high school, I was officially sworn in as a firefighter for the same department my family had been part of for over 100 years.

The abuse left me scarred and angry.

The training was hard, and I learned a lot about respect, discipline, and following orders. Although most of this was already drilled into my brain from a young age, learning from instructors who had been family friends for years made this feel more purposeful.

Right out of the gate, I had my first fire—the same night as being sworn in. It was a "small" fire, and the details don't matter. What does matter is what happened at the end when things were winding down. Between the adrenaline of being inside a burning building, and the hard work, the team, and camaraderie, I finally found my identity.

I found self-esteem and confidence, a purpose.

All of this came in the form of a uniform and badge, strengthened by the love of my brother firefighters. I finally belonged to something beyond my messed-up family. I loved it all and threw myself into the career with my heart and soul.

I ended up going to college to obtain a degree in Fire Science, along with earning my EMT certification right after high school. While doing this, I remained an "on-call" member of the fire department. This meant that, like a volunteer firefighter, I didn't "live" at the fire station for 24 hours at a time. I worked short day shifts here and there, maybe bad weather coverage, but usually only responded to my fire station when alerted by a pager I wore on my belt, along with monitoring the police scanner.

It was clear right from the get-go that I was what the fire service termed a "black cloud." In my case this meant a lot of fires and bad calls. Growing up in a firefighting family, I was aware of the inevitable array of bad shit I was going to see. What I wasn't prepared for was *how* it was going to affect me and how some of it would re-open the wounds of my past.

> *Through firefighting I found self-esteem and confidence... a purpose.*

While still in college and working a separate part-time job, I met a girl. *The* girl, actually. We fell in love and had a few bumps in the road, but eventually got married in September of 2000. I was only 22 and my wife, Heather, was 23. By June of 2002, we had two kids and owned a home in a small city in central Massachusetts. I was full-time in private EMS on an ambulance, working in larger cities, along with pulling shifts at the firehouse. Occasionally I had side jobs running training courses at the fire department, and tried to find time to be a husband and father.

I was burning both ends of the candle to avoid dealing with my demons, which were trying their hardest to win me over. I had nightmares, outbursts, flashbacks, hypervigilance, and I was constantly on alert at a "ten." We tried to get me what help existed back then, but it didn't do much.

Spring 2003, Heather and I hit a few major bumps. One involved me being arrested. The two of us separated for a few weeks. At the end of that time, we tried to mend our relationship by going out with another couple who were our closest friends.

It was Friday, April 11, 2003.

What began as a night of forgiveness and moving on, became one of the most traumatic experiences of my life. Shortly after leaving our house, we got in a car accident on the highway. I was knocked unconscious, and Heather was killed. Our two friends received minor injuries. I spent the night in the intensive care unit, down the hall from my wife who was being kept "alive" via a dozen different machines.

She was gone.

The next morning, following all the formalities regarding my now deceased wife, I was tasked with a new, even more horrible and daunting mission. I had to go and explain to my two-year old son and his 10-month-old sister that their mother was never coming home.

This event, coupled with my childhood, family dynamic, and a reoccurring onslaught of bad emergencies on the job, became the beginning of my downward spiral. During the months immediately following the accident I drank, drugged, and deprived myself of sleep and rest. I constantly felt I needed to be punished because I had been driving the night of the accident when my wife died. Most of the time I just didn't want to feel anything. For a good amount of time, I didn't.

What began as a night of forgiveness became the most traumatic experience of my life.

Eventually my abuse of drugs and alcohol tapered off, but I had already moved into a different addiction. Sex. Dozens of women came and went from my life, either nightly or over a period of a few months. The one consistency was my inability or desire to commit to anything. I felt as if nothing was worth striving for in the long term.

My work ethic also suffered. My health started failing with my constant anxiety, hypervigilance, and bouts of depression and anger. I began having chest pain and other related cardiac issues. Worst of all, my relationships were all falling apart, especially with my children Zack and Morgyn.

I no longer cared about anything. I became a cold, emotionless person. On the surface, nothing seemed to affect or even bother me. I never appeared overly happy or even smiled. On the inside I was dying. My heart and soul were bleeding and even with all my years on the job as a firefighter and EMT, I couldn't seem to stop it.

I lost custody of my kids in 2010, during the first of several psychiatric hospitalizations. A few years prior, the kids and I had moved into a big house with my mother and step-father. During the process of taking parental custody from me, my mother and Heather's mother decided to kick me out of the house.

I became homeless.

The week of Thanksgiving that year I was terminated from my ambulance job for one of the cities I worked for. They cited excessive absenteeism, conduct, and an overall bad behavior as their reasons. The fire department I served was also at their wits end with my shit. It wasn't uncommon for me to bark off at those in higher rank and even to the chief from time to time. Of course, I was living a nightmare of literally everything in my life either disappearing or ending abruptly.

I was angry *all the time.*

I was unapproachable *all the time.*

And I was quickly becoming unreliable *all the time.*

I just wanted it all to end. I didn't want to die, necessarily, but I didn't want to exist. I felt like a burden and embarrassment to every single person in my life, both personally and professionally.

By spring 2011, riddled with constant guilt and shame, I'd made five suicide attempts since my first at age 13. I was mis-diagnosed with bipolar disorder, and given over a dozen different medications to try to control my emotions and actions. During what can be looked at as failed therapy, I never admitted to my childhood trauma, especially being raped. The job I had been doing since age 18 was never brought into the equation. PTSD was something only soldiers got diagnosed with, and even that was a new thing at the time.

I just wanted to end it all.

I met a woman while working for a new ambulance service in Worcester, Massachusetts. Adele was 12 years younger than me but for some reason we hit it off, and age never seemed to be a factor. She picked up right away that there was some serious shit lying below the surface of who and what was Keith Hanks.

Still, when we began sleeping in the same bed and eventually living together, I tried to keep as much from her as I could. Fast forward a few years, and we became engaged to be married.

In fall 2013, I reestablished contact with my biological father and we began mending our past. Unfortunately he was already riddled with cancer, and due to the chemo treatments, had a very bad cardiac condition. If he wasn't having an actual heart attack, he would have angina. If it wasn't heart related, he would be sick, weak, and tired from all the cancer treatments.

Eventually all of this caught up with him and he passed away in June of 2014, about 6 weeks before my wedding to Adele. I was there when he took his last breath, following a heart attack at home.

This became the catalyst for my buried symptoms to bubble to the surface. By 2015, I needed help. My fire department sent me to a first responder retreat of sorts where I learned I may have PTSD. After leaving treatment there, I ended up at McLean Hospital, just outside of Boston, where I was officially diagnosed with Complex-PTSD.

This diagnosis came from the sheer number of traumas I had been through and was able to finally admit to, specifically my childhood trauma and rape. This gave us hope. Now stood the task of correctly helping me heal and move on.

The healing didn't come fast enough for some in my life and spelled the end of my career as a firefighter and EMT. In 2016, after two decades as a firefighter, I left the fire service. The following fall, I left private EMS work on the ambulance. Twenty-one years had been spent giving selfless service to community and country.

> *The healing didn't come fast enough.*

Because it was mental-health related, along with a few other circumstances, there was no formal goodbye.

No retirement parties.

No gold badge, or service plaque presentation.

Not even a "Thank you for your service."

I was simply cast out. Since age 18, I'd had an identity and thought I knew my purpose in life. The badge, the uniform, and the job defined who I had been, and now at age 39 without any of that, I became lost with no direction.

Adele tried her hardest to assure me this was just a fork in the road, "an opportunity to find my true self."

I was miserable. Most of my friends had come through my job—fire service, police, or EMS. A lot of those folks did an about face when word got out that I had retired and was going on disability for PTSD.

I've always felt a sense of satisfaction from working with my hands, an instant gratification that likely stems from "putting the wet stuff on the red stuff" as a firefighter. So, I started to do woodworking and light carpentry. Small projects filled my newfound free time.

In 2018, Adele was working full-time as an ER nurse. She and I bought a house after years of jumping from one apartment to the next. I was working through a significant amount of past traumas with an amazing doctor and therapist at McLean's.

Due to Adele's diagnosis of Lupus, we had always been told pregnancy would be a risk. Come fall 2018 we received the medical "OK" to get pregnant and did so in a matter of weeks! Our original due date happened to be the same as our five-year wedding anniversary—August 8, 2019.

As summer 2019 began, we quickly realized we would likely not make it to our original due date. Long story extremely abridged, after leaving for her 3:00 PM to 3:00 AM shift in the ER one afternoon, I received a frantic phone call from my wife. Her blood pressure had gone through the roof. She was being admitted to the labor and delivery unit at the hospital where she worked.

Adele began hemorrhaging blood along with other problems. Concerns arose for not only her but our unborn child.

The decision was made to move her to a higher-level hospital for treatment. The next few hours were awful, and I was convinced I was about to be faced with burying another wife *and* a child I would never get to meet or fall in love with and raise.

After some time of uncertainty, a visit to the hospital chapel, and a lot of prayers, my daughter Riley made her entrance to the world on July 2, which happened to also be Adele's birthday. Relatively unscathed, Riley needed less attention than my wife.

After almost three weeks in the NICU, we were all home and beginning the process of moving on and becoming a family unit. Unbeknownst to most, I spiraled downward at an astronomical rate. Come that December, I was in one of the darkest places I had ever been. One fateful night, after I told Adele I loved her, we joked for a while and smiled and hugged as she walked out the door for work.

Then I walked down to our basement.

I pulled out one of my handguns. Loaded the magazine into it. Put it against my head and pulled the trigger.

It clicked, and for a few moments I thought it was all over and I was free of all the pain, guilt, and shame that tormented me for decades.

Obviously, it did not.

What it did accomplish was create a turning point in my life. Not immediately though. After a two-month hospitalization that included more intense therapy, group talks, activities, and some invasive procedures, I finally broke free of the massive depression that caused me to almost end my life for the sixth time.

The growth I experienced from that time forward was previously unparalleled. I found a new lease on life and a sense of direction. I finally started making concrete decisions about what I wanted to do moving forward.

I decided to take all my pain, my fears, my failures and tragedies, and show others hope.

I began pushing for advocacy through social media. I put more effort into writing my memoirs which had become almost 165,000 words, and something I wanted to make a published book. Then, in the middle of the COVID-19 pandemic, I received an opportunity to tell my story in a way I had never done before.

In July 2021, at the New Hampshire Fire Academy, I stood in front of over 75 of my brother and sister first responders and gave my first live presentation. That following September, I did the same at a first responder mental health symposium with almost 200 in attendance.

I became even more motivated, determined, and disciplined in my mission to turn the tide on PTSD and suicide in the first responder community. Things took off in an astronomical way from there on out. Before I knew it, I was being asked to be part of a life coaching business as the "street cred" and voice of change. I quickly received coaching, my coach certification, and eventually became the Director of Promotions at this business designed specifically for first responders and their families.

> *My mission is to turn the tide on PTSD and suicide in the first responder community.*

By combining what I had learned through coaching and years of trauma-focused therapy, I moved out of my comfort zone. I read *a lot* of books, including self-help, meditation, spirituality, and power of the brain books which opened my eyes to a bigger picture.

This bigger picture quickly became my motivation with the goal of changing the world's view and treatment of mental health and wellness. I pushed harder. I wrote and spoke deeper. My determination reached never before obtained levels. Before I knew it, I was helping to produce and star in a feature length documentary based on my life with PTSD. Sixteen friends, family, and former co-workers were interviewed. Soon after filming finished, I was asked to appear in two other films, along with numerous resource videos on the subject.

I began speaking at venues in different parts of the country and on podcasts as far away as Australia. My love for writing and sharing my thoughts, feelings, and experiences through the written word also took off. Before I knew it, I was being asked to write for an ongoing book series (this one), and I submitted an article for an international forum—*Fire Engineering Magazine*. Shortly after that another publication caught wind of my abilities and asked me to write for them. My own book has reaped the benefits of this resiliency, determination, and refusal to give up, and will hopefully soon see publication.

My marriage is back on track. I'm a good father and love the time I get with my youngest daughter. I'm more open, empathetic, and most importantly I feel the full spectrum of my emotions.

There was a time when I was surrounded by darkness, with seemingly no way out. Often, I couldn't see the light at all and there was little hope of success.

These days, I'm guided by the light, determination, and knowledge that there is hope. Yes, at times the darkness still appears and tries its hardest to overwhelm the light and hope. But I survive and push forward because the fire inside me burns brighter than the flames around me.

There is always hope. Much love.

Keith Hanks

KEITH HANKS is a retired Firefighter and EMT who dedicated 21 years of his life to the service of others. He serviced his community as a training officer, certified educator, and field training officer. Keith worked both inner-city EMS as well as fire. Like many in the first responder community, the job had its cost. From childhood trauma and sexual abuse to traumatic calls and the passing of his first wife, Keith has faced many trials and tragedies that resulted in self-harm, substance abuse, lies, and multiple suicide attempts. After decades of damage, Keith began to put the pieces of his life back together.

Keith was diagnosed with Complex PTSD in 2015. The job, the service, and his dedication caused this injury, and consequently his retirement. What PTSD didn't change was the love and devotion to his community and to his fellow first responders. Keith has since dedicated his life to advocating for mental illness, substance and alcohol abuse recovery, and suicide awareness. Since starting this mission, Keith built an international support group through Facebook for First Responders and Veterans for PTSD and other job-related mental health issues. Keith was asked to be a part of the Deconstructing Stigma Project and has a billboard that hangs in the International Terminal at Logan Airport in Boston, Massachusetts.

In March 2022, he completed the filming of his first feature-length documentary focusing on PTSD in the first responder community, and has since been featured in two other related documentaries.

Keith is a national speaker, podcast personality, and published author. He is a contributing author at *Fire Engineering* magazine and The Volunteer Firefighter forum.

Transparency in his own life has led him to share his story to reach the most people he can. He is known for saying that his life goal is to reduce suicide in the first responder community through education, support resources, and to make it "OK to not be OK." Keith is currently a life coach and was fundamental in the start-up of First Responder Coaching as the Director of Business Development, and then Director of Promotions. He also created, hosted, and produced the Resilient Responder Podcast.

He resides in New Hampshire with his wife and is the proud father of three incredible children.

Facebook: @keith.hanks.5

Instagram: @khanksmz

Twitter: @khanksmz78

LinkedIn: @keith-hanks-44218b229

YouTube: @keithhanks2333

The Story You Try Hardest Not to Tell

Lori Ann Hood

As a young mother myself, I cannot fathom making the same choices my adopted parents did. For years I suffered fear, loneliness, neglect, secrets, and lies. I would never wish my first 19 years of life on anyone. In time I've forgiven the main people who were involved, setting myself free from their control, but the internal scars and memories can't be forgotten. I learned early in life that hatred often comes from those who hold titles and smile in public, but the worst happens behind closed doors.

My life of horror began before I knew my adopted parents. My older twin brothers had heart problems that our drunken father, who was a truck driver, didn't know how to handle. His addiction caused their health issues to be met with physical violence and neglect.

When I was 3 years old, my brothers and I were not only taken from our violent father but we were also ripped away from some of the most loving people God put in our path—the only loving hands we knew, church members who offered my dad food and other stuff. An unfair foster system permanently separated me and my siblings. One of my brothers got put into a group home and was deemed unadoptable. The other went to a foster home and got adopted by a single father. I myself went through several foster homes before going to the final home of horrors.

A 5-year-old confused, sad, distraught, and angry little blue-eyed blonde-haired girl thought she was finally safe. The 14 years that followed were anything but that.

A new home, new surroundings, new friends, and a new school just weren't the best for my troubled soul. In fact I repeated kindergarten because not only was I mentally behind but emotionally as well. On top of the hatred at the hands of my biological father, it quickly came from my adopted dad as well.

Both my adopted parents were very much about using their money for themselves. In public, we were a family that had everything and was adored by so many others, but behind closed doors there was black and blue, and my dad did unimaginable things to me. Eventually we got my younger sister from foster care as well and I was terrified for her. Two years younger than me, I wanted to keep her safe. Heartbreakingly I wasn't always able to.

My sister and I could've been very close, but our parents pitted us against each other. The comparisons and more created a distance. We had some good moments, but it was hard to make them last. When our parents were asleep at the other end of the house, I would hold her hand and rub her hair to help her fall asleep. Like all sisters, we had secrets we never told our parents. But we also lied to others and hid the horrors of what we experienced.

> *Not only was I mentally behind, but emotionally as well.*

When I was in the seventh grade, our family moved from a friendly neighborhood full of kids our age, way out to the lonely countryside. My sister and I didn't have to share a room anymore, but that created a strain on our closeness. Our father went to great lengths to do what he did and not let others know. It was easier in this new house. He could sneak me away to do everything he wanted. To say my sister and I got into trouble with boys early is an understatement. She became a mom at age 15. Somehow this became my fault and I got punished.

In high school, things seemed to line up in a way that gave me a fighting chance. As a freshman, I joined FFA and got exposed to others who put the pieces of my home life together. During my sophomore year I became a cheerleader. These activities kept me away from home and brought amazing people into my life, friends with bonds that to this day are still very present.

In English class, writing assignments became a form of needed therapy that helped me thrive. I fell in love with creative writing, and learned how poetry and stories can both hide and reveal information at the same time. I used this to my advantage and am grateful I had a teacher who knew what I was trying to say.

In my third year of high school, I was looking for an elective class to fill my schedule. The English teacher from the previous year offered a creative writing class and I signed up for it. Through those assignments I found safety in sharing the hidden parts of my life without putting my teacher at risk as a mandated reporter. The facts didn't evade her though. While she gave me a safe space to write and use her class as therapy, she also created a safe environment. Should I lose all my inner strength and need an absolute way out, I had one set up and a safe plan to make it all happen quickly.

> *Through creative writing, I found safety in sharing the hidden parts of my life.*

It was this year that truly gave me the inner fight I needed to keep going forward. The librarian showed me a way to write and save all my assignments so that my parents at home wouldn't have access to it to ruin it. My cheer coaches knew so much and tried their very best to help and support in any way possible.

My last year of high school was the absolute worst. My parents didn't let me have any of the normal monumental moments. As a protective sibling, there were so many things I tolerated from our father so that he would leave my sister alone. It worked for a while, until he realized I was leaving soon and went after her the same way.

My sister was braver than I ever was. She said something to a trusted adult. Since our father was a respected member of the community, he was able to lie his way out of it, but realized he was losing his hold.

At 18 years old I finally found my escape. The U.S. Army recruiter called my house and told me of the opportunity the Army could be. As tired and miserable as I was, I was desperate and took it.

My parents were angry, but I was thoroughly protected from abuse then. I had an absolute way out. And because of their own decisions, even my future finances became outside of their control. I had foiled their plans for all future manipulation. All I had to do was keep going forward with the goal in mind. And I did this well to the bitter end.

For years, I tried not to think about what I had gone through. Self-harm, addictions, eating disorders, therapy, and medicine didn't help. I hated my body, hated myself, and I had no confidence. I was always in fight or flight mode.

The summer before basic training was the longest and most miserable summer of my life. I finally got on the plane—the first one of my life—and took a shallow breath of freedom. But I had to go back to that house for Christmas and it was horrible. On December 26, 2010, I walked out their door for the last time.

I hated my body, hated myself...

In the Army, I met someone and we quickly become a couple. It was against so many rules for us to be together and yet we continued. I left the Army with him, as we were both severely injured and unable to continue to train for the jobs we really wanted. He and I were engaged already, so I went home with him, cross-country, to his family. To this day I do not regret that choice.

At first our relationship was happy and healthy and absolutely amazing. We had a baby shortly after our third anniversary of being engaged. She was born with Down Syndrome. He was in college pursuing his passion of being a mechanic so I stayed at home and took care of our baby.

When she was about two years old, our relationship turned toxic. But I didn't have any family and he had alienated all my friends. I was stuck. It got to the point where he always spoke negatively to me, never a positive thing to say. Everything I did, said, wanted, or needed was wrong. After six and a half long years together, we called it quits.

He was so toxic he made me move out of his grandparents' house where we were living, on my birthday, which was also Father's Day that year. I moved in with a friend who then abandoned me in her house. Shortly after that, I lost two dear people back to back to tragic deaths.

This started my first big spiral as an adult. No one understood the mental struggles I was going through. I needed to face all the horrible things that had happened to me. While I was starting to find solid ground, roommates put me in a dangerous situation where the unthinkable became part of my life again just before New Year's. I was never okay with the manipulation but I needed a roof over my head.

Shortly after that I moved in with a different friend. This person had some not so great coping mechanisms though, which I quickly fell prey to as well. Fear, lies, secrets, guys' attention... quickly these became my life again, and I stayed stuck for a couple months in a vicious cycle. I was mentally and emotionally worn out, not coping with anything in healthy ways.

About four months after being attacked at New Year's, I was left alone with a friend of a friend, who was messed up on addictions. Yet another man with bad intentions regarding my body.

I needed an environment shift. I wasn't looking for a boyfriend, but found a good friend. He and I talked a lot and finally met in person at my friend's house. The very next day, my friend's mom kicked me out, so I moved in with my new friend and his roommate.

> *I needed an environment shift.*

He and I made some unwise decisions and I became pregnant with my second child, his first. Due to safety concerns, he and I made the decision to move into his mom's house. After being there for a few months, I became deathly ill and started a long three-month journey of being in and out of hospitals.

I ended up having surgery to remove my gallbladder, and then had fatal hidden preeclampsia. I gave birth to my youngest six weeks early. It was a long road to recovery and I dipped back into depression. With the help of his mom and step-dad, I pulled out of it and finally truly started healing from the trauma I'd gone through.

Amid all the chaos and aftermath, I found my voice and began writing again. Some amazing supportive people made all the difference for me. I made the decision to put all my poetry on a public blog, where I found my story was not only echoed but an inspiration. The poetry of my past struggles showed others that no matter what happens, better things are ahead if you just keep going.

The emails I received from others who read my poems truly made me proud... but also broke my heart. I started to share my story to various other audiences and it became its own form of healing.

With help from amazing people along the way, writing and music have truly been a form of therapy for me. I know it's hard to reach out and ask for help when you feel like nobody else understands, but it's worth it. So many doors to healing can be opened, not only for yourself, but also to help others to heal.

Sharing my story is its own form of healing.

The story you try hardest not to tell can be the biggest blessing for someone else. Even when it feels like you're all alone, you're not. If you relate at all to my story, I'm sorry... but also know that I'm so proud of you for waking up today and keeping up the fight.

LORI ANN HOOD

"The best way out is always through." —Robert Frost

LORI ANN HOOD lives in South Carolina and is the mother of two with special needs. She got into writing at a young age but didn't lean into it until high school. While learning to harness the art of writing, words and music became her favorite forms of therapy. Her dream is to speak on stages to help others with her story of overcoming trauma. The scariest thing (outside of leaving the only home she knew for 14 years) was posting her autobiographical poetry on a public blog site. She never intended to be the light in others' darkness, but she's glad it happened. No one should feel alone in this world.

Read her poetry:
www.poetrypoem.com/sassylo

Instagram:
www.instagram.com/sassylo_1991_

BEAUTY FOR ASHES

KARYN HARPER

Hope for Your Future

NO MATTER WHAT HAPPENS IN YOUR LIFE, no matter what you've been through, there is hope. You are going to be okay. There is absolutely nothing that can happen to you that you can't get through.

This story, Beauty for Ashes, shares the same title as a song by Christian artist Crystal Lewis, and a therapeutic book by Joyce Meyers that really helped me in dealing with my abuse issues.

Where I Began

The first verse of Lewis's song talks about how sorrow is always around. My entire life, sorrow has surrounded me. From childhood I just couldn't seem to get away from it, no matter how hard I tried. I didn't fit in anywhere. It never felt like I belonged. I was too different even though I tried so hard and was willing to do just about anything to be accepted.

Many times I made myself the laughing stock because I thought that would get people to like me. But, of course, it didn't. People didn't even pity me. Instead, they seemed disgusted by me. I basically had no friends. The ones I did have were really just acquaintances. Nobody really knew me. Except Tracy. And I didn't see her often. It was incredibly isolating and painful.

The "black sheep," it used to hurt and bother me that I didn't fit in, even with my own family, and that I am so different from them. But I have come to terms with it and accepted it.

The hardest thing while growing up was the lack of emotional support. My anger scared me. I acted out often, and was consistently in trouble for losing my temper.

I also was an anxious child. I never talked about it because I didn't know what it was. In all honesty, I still don't really talk about it. Most of my friends have no idea how I struggle with social anxiety, because I don't outwardly appear anxious. They can't see the huge pit inside me. My nerves are frazzled, my muscles are all in a ball, and my brain is running a thousand miles a minute. I can socialize for a period of time, but once I hit my limit, I'm gone. No apologies and no explanations.

Depression and suicidal thoughts were my constant companions by the time I was ten years old. As a teenager, mood swings went out of my control. I was scared, my family was scared. We had no idea what was going on with me. We knew nothing about mental illness. It definitely wasn't publicized like it is today. It wasn't even spoken about because it was a taboo subject. Nobody understood it, so nobody wanted to deal with it.

No matter what you've been through, there is hope.

People are afraid of what they don't understand. Even now, with all of the progress we've made, there is still stigma surrounding mental illness. Growing up with an undiagnosed mental illness was torture and left emotional scars that may never go away.

Today I understand that my parents did the best they could with what they had to work with. They simply didn't know how to help me—or that I even needed help. I do not blame them for not giving me the emotional support I needed. I wasn't able to express my own emotions or feelings safely. I had no one to go to with any of the overwhelming thoughts that consumed my mind. I didn't have a healthy outlet. Therefore, I began looking for other ways to deal with everything.

The funny thing about finding ways to escape pain and suffering is that the pain and suffering are still right there waiting for you when you can't run anymore. For a person with an addictive personality like me, any means of escape can be dangerous. For me, it was almost fatal.

Daily Drinking

By the time I was 23 I was a daily drinker, which consisted of getting completely wasted every night of the week until I blacked out. I couldn't hold down a job, couldn't pay my rent, and I had no real friends. My family was afraid to be around me. Nothing mattered to me except where I was going to get my next drink/drug.

> *People are afraid of what they don't understand.*

I woke up thinking about how I would get drunk or high that day, and who had money. Because I never did. I was the town bar whore. I did whatever I had to do to get what I needed.

In five short years, alcohol became my master. I no longer enjoyed drinking... instead I drank to survive. I literally couldn't live without it.

In August of 2000, I took my last drink. That night, I crashed a wedding reception, got into a fight with the bride, and refused to leave the reception. They gave up. So, of course, I got wasted.

Hitting Bottom

Drinking nearly killed me. When I came to, I was on a wooden swing covered in all of my bodily fluids and drowning in my own vomit.

The next day I began the process of detoxing at my parents' house, and within a week I was in a rehab facility.

Today I thank God because that night opened my eyes to the problem I had. I knew I needed help. In rehab, I began attending AA meetings, and I am an active member of AA still today.

Sex Equaled Attention

I can't tell the story of my life and leave out the biggest trauma. Around the age of 13, I found that sex would get me attention, even if it was only for a short time. I began to use sex as a weapon to get the things I wanted in life. And it was a powerful tool.

Most of the time it got me what I thought I wanted. I used this very tool to feed my drug and alcohol addiction. But, as with most tools, if you're not careful, it can and will be used against you. That was definitely my experience.

When I was around 24, a guy I'll call "John Doe" came into my life. We met through his sister, and we began partying together. Of course, we also began sleeping together. And, eventually, he moved in with me.

At first, he was kind, quiet, and a gentleman. But when he drank and got high, he became a very different person. He was mean, full of rage, and extremely abusive. Like me, he got high and drunk every day. I simply became a punching bag and a blow-up doll that he was able to have sex with.

I became terrified of him, and so did my friends. They stopped coming over to party because they were so afraid of him. No one was willing to get involved for fear of retaliation. I even begged them not to say anything to anyone because I was terrified of his reaction.

I ended up getting pregnant. I was so happy. I wanted that child with every fiber in my being. I couldn't wait to be a mother and to hold my child in my arms. I dreamed about what it would be like raising this child. I was going to have the baby, with or without a father... preferably without, all things considered.

John Doe simply would not believe that my child belonged to him. The beatings intensified. For the sake of my child, I finally got up the courage to kick him out, and I took his key.

That night, he broke in while I was sleeping. He dragged me out of bed and began my last beating. He punched and kicked me in the stomach. When I tried to fight back, he pulled out a knife and began stabbing me in the stomach. He continued until I lost the baby.

He murdered my child. He ripped away my chance to fulfill the dream of becoming a mother and raising a child. He left me lying in a pool of blood, unconscious. Praise God, when a co-worker came to pick me up for work the next day and I didn't answer the door, she got concerned and looked in the window. She couldn't see me, but she saw the blood and called 911 immediately.

Paramedics told her that if she hadn't come when she did, I would not have survived. This was what it finally took to get me out of that situation for good.

Denial Is Powerful

You might think this experience would have been enough to wake me up and realize that I had a problem... problems, actually... that I needed help to overcome. But it was not. Instead it made me more fiercely determined to prove that I was a strong woman and didn't need help from anyone else. "I got this. I will do me, because ain't nobody else gonna do it for me, or do it right anyway."

So I continued using drugs, alcohol, and men to escape from the reality of life. I honestly believed my life was normal. I thought everyone drank/drugged and lived like I did. If someone actually had the guts to tell me I had a problem, then I just blew them off. I cared about no one but myself. I did whatever I had to do to get what I wanted, without any care for how my actions affected others.

In the song "Beauty for Ashes," it talks about how there is always hope for a better future, if we trust God and believe His Word. Through Christ, wholeness and healing are available.

Healing Is Possible for Me

I never believed that healing was possible for me. I didn't think I would ever feel whole. I thought I would always have that vacuum in my soul. I tried filling that void with everything I could find, and it all just left me feeling alone and empty.

Today, thanks to Alcoholics Anonymous and the twelve-step program, I have found wholeness and so much healing. I actually have a relationship with God today that I am comfortable with.

Today I look back at my life and see how, all along, God was with me. He has always been there. I am the one who chose to separate myself from Him. God saved my life and protected me so many times when I was out there doing my own thing. But I couldn't see it. All that time, He was carrying me.

Today I wholeheartedly believe that God is always with me, guiding and directing me in this journey we call life. I believe the truth the Bible tells me, that He will never leave me nor forsake me. No matter what. He *sees* me, He *hears* me, He *knows* me. Inside and out. *All* of my parts. And somehow, He still chooses to love me unconditionally. That blows my mind. God is *so* good!

Guilt, Shame, and Recovery

The things I have done when I was under the influence of drugs and alcohol, and the people I have hurt, haunted me for such a long time. Even in sobriety. I didn't believe I could ever really be forgiven for all of the awful things I did. I couldn't forgive myself, let alone believe someone else could forgive me.

That guilt and shame kept me sick. There was no way I could possibly move on to become the beautiful woman God created me to be as long as I stayed stuck in that shame. I finally had to learn how to hang up the bloody sledgehammer and stop beating myself up for my past—and even for my current character defects... abusing myself and continuing to listen to negative thoughts that tell me I'm not worthy, I'm not good enough, I will never measure up...

Guilt and shame kept me sick.

I had to silence those voices by learning the truth. And then by repeating the truth to myself every time those shameful voices re-emerge. Which is often.

Never mind the fear. Fear dominated me. It infected every single part of me. It controlled my decisions, my actions, and my thoughts. And it still can, if I allow it to.

Choices

I have a choice today. I can:

> **F**orget
>
> **E**verything
>
> **A**nd
>
> **R**un

...or I can:

> **F**ace
>
> **E**verything
>
> **A**nd
>
> **R**ecover...

Just for today, I am choosing to face everything and recover. It's complicated! It's not easy, and it takes a lot of hard work. But it is worth it!

Fear Never Entirely Goes Away

On that note, I want to say here that writing this... my truth, my story... has been incredibly difficult. I have had to work through many fears while putting this together for the world to see.

It's one thing to stand in front of your church and share your testimony, somewhere you're surrounded by loved ones and people who know you well.

It's a completely different thing to put your story in print where absolutely anyone can read it.

Talk about not having control over how others respond! I had, and still have, a fear that my family will not receive my story well, or that I may unintentionally hurt a family member. I mean, even my family doesn't know my whole story.

There is also fear in simply knowing that once my story is out there, in print, I can't take it back. I can't take back anything I have said.

Truth Overpowers Fear

One of the most powerful truths I have learned is that truth overpowers fear. Once a word is spoken out loud, or printed on paper and received by another person, there's no way to take those words back. I can apologize and make amends if I have hurt someone with my words, but I can't erase the hurt my words caused.

So it is my responsibility to do my best to be kind and intentional with my words. I have tried not to say things that are unnecessary. I try to be to the point in a gentle way. Because that is how I respond best to others.

Forgiveness Required

In regards to forgiveness, I feel like I could write an entire chapter. Forgiveness is hard. Plain and simple. And the deeper the hurt, the harder forgiveness becomes.

Before I got sober, forgiveness was not even a word in my vocabulary. I had no capacity to forgive. I didn't understand forgiveness. I didn't know that forgiveness is *not* about the person who hurt me. I forgive because it frees *me!*

When I got sober, I was full of hatred and resentment. I hated the world. But more importantly, I hated myself. I simply could not believe there was forgiveness available to someone like me. Then I began working the Twelve Steps of AA. The principles and the promises of AA changed my life. But I want to specifically talk about how the program taught me about real and lasting forgiveness.

Forgiveness Is Freedom from Bondage

In the back of the book *Alcoholics Anonymous*, there are some personal stories written by alcoholics in recovery. I learned about deep and lasting forgiveness from one of these stories, titled "Freedom from Bondage."

In this story, the writer says,

> "If you have a resentment you want to be free of, if you will pray for the person or the thing that you resent, you will be free. If you will ask in prayer for everything you want for yourself to be given to them, you will be free. Ask for their health, their prosperity, their happiness, and you will be free. Even when you don't really want it for them and your prayers are only words and you don't really mean it, go ahead and do it anyway. Do it every day for two weeks, and you will find you have come to mean it and to want it for them, and you will realize that where you used to feel bitterness and resentment and hatred, you now feel compassionate understanding and love."

I came to a place in my own sobriety where I was faced with the realization that I had to be rid of my own hatred and resentment, or I was no doubt going to drink again. I didn't want to drink again. So I decided to give this forgiveness thing a try.

Even though I didn't really believe it would work, what did I have to lose? I was willing to try anything. I began praying for John Doe—the person I had the deepest hatred for. At first, it did seem fake because I didn't mean a word of it. I didn't want him to have *anything* good. But I kept doing it. I'm not sure exactly how long I had to do this, but it was a lot longer than two weeks. I also know that I kept doing it anyway.

This prayer works every time.

The longer I prayed for him, the more I began to actually mean what I was saying. Eventually, without even realizing it had happened, I saw that I had begun to genuinely forgive John Doe. That doesn't mean he hadn't hurt me, and it didn't take away the pain of my loss. It simply means that he no longer controlled me through my own hatred. He was no longer getting free rent in my head. And I was finally able to feel the pain, grieve the loss, and live free of this resentment.

I, too, was no longer in bondage. I have used this prayer for many resentments, and I can honestly say it works every time. I have remained sober. Eventually, the resentment fades and forgiveness is born.

Mental Illness and Recovery

I cannot share my story without talking about my recovery from mental illness. When I introduce myself in an AA meeting, I say that I am a grateful *recovered* alcoholic. And, just now, in response to having the courage to speak my truth in this book—that can be read by absolutely anyone in the world—I have had a wonderful realization.

I can also honestly say that I am a grateful *recovered* person with mental illness.

What an incredible epiphany! I just can't put into words how free I feel at this moment. To be able to use the word *recovered* in connection with my mental illness is absolutely huge!

Now, I know that word is going to bring up questions for some, and others may wonder exactly what I mean when I say I've recovered from mental illness. That's a great question!

What I mean is that I have recovered from the hopeless state of mind and body.

Hopelessness has defined my life, especially when it comes to my mental health. I had no faith that I would ever be free from that hopelessness. I simply could not see any light at the end of the tunnel. There was barely even a trace of light to my current location, let alone at the end of a tunnel.

But because I was able to finally see and admit I had a problem—and take the very scary step of asking for help—I have been set free! I have the tools I need today to overcome the incredibly loud voices in my head that tell me lies like:

"You're stupid."

"Your story doesn't even matter."

"You have nothing to say that anyone else wants to hear."

"You're not worthy."

"Your family is never going to forgive you for this."

Those lies don't limit me today!

Today, my life is defined in simply knowing that I am a child of God. He created me and is continuing to mold me into the beautiful woman He has always intended for me to be. What God says of me today is the only definition I need in life.

There is no better way for me to end this chapter about my life than by returning to the song "Beauty for Ashes." The bridge and chorus talk about being lost and how God found me and set me free from the bondage of this world. When God looks at me today, He actually sees me as pure and clean! That is still hard for me to wrap my head around. But I believe it to be true.

God has taken the ashes of my life and turned them into something truly beautiful. He has replaced my fears with strength, my mourning with gladness, and my utter despair with a real sense of peace and serenity.

God can do this for you, too.

Karyn Harper

KARYN HARPER was born and raised in Northeastern Ohio and now lives in Rochester, New York. She is an avid football fan and a diehard member of Steeler Nation until the day she dies. She is also a big fan of hockey, and of course, the Pens.

She loves music and is a member of the music team at her church. She is passionate about advocating for support for people suffering with mental health and addiction issues and getting the message out that there is hope for a better life... a future.

TELL SOMEONE

ERIK DAROSA

Hiding in plain sight for all the world to see
Hoping like hell they never figure out me
Chasing me down alleyways these thoughts won't let me be
No matter how hard I try I just can't seem to break free
Today marks the start of a brand new day
I'm steppin' out into the world
There's no more hidin' in the shadows for me
My secret's gonna be revealed

—*"Shadows" by Erik DaRosa*

FOR AS LONG AS I CAN REMEMBER, I have been deemed "okay" according to society's definition. Yet I've experienced everything from the fear of sleeping as a young child, to the onset of terrifying intrusive thoughts as an adolescent, to the ever-worsening panic attacks and paralyzing anxiety throughout my high school and college years. This all culminated in a debilitating dissociative episode as an adult in the late summer of 2004.

Everyone Thought I Was Thriving, Including Me

Looking back now, from my 51-year-old adult and better-equipped perspective, I can see all the triggers and related physical and emotional manifestations. For some reason, I did everything to hide my "not okay-ness" from the world. I chose what felt like the path of least resistance, the same path that far too many people choose: to suffer in silence. For decades I outwardly displayed a façade—that of a usually smiling, highly functioning, type-A successful overachiever. I had, subconsciously or not, chosen to accept society's stigma rather than embrace my true self and the vulnerability that came with it. And during that time I never felt strong enough to stand solidly on my own two feet.

If I'm being brutally honest, I spent the first 33 years of my life without a voice and afraid to remove the mask behind which I had been hiding since I was 7.

> *I have been deemed "okay" according to society's definition.*

Years of crippling anxiety had left me feeling unsafe, insecure, and out of control. I battled with Harm obsessive-compulsive disorder (OCD), which led to intrusive thoughts as my constant co-pilot during waking hours. The countless checking rituals I performed to keep me "safe" from the boogeymen left me overwhelmed and exhausted, with little time to be a kid. For decades I kept telling myself I was different from everyone else; I told myself I was broken and the only one. If I had only known the truth.

To be sure we're on the same page, let's stop and look at what OCD and intrusive thoughts are. According to the American Psychiatric Association's *Diagnostic and Statistical Manual of Mental Disorders, Fifth Edition (DSM-5)*, OCD is defined as recurrent and persistent thoughts, urges or images that are experienced, at some time during the disturbance, as intrusive, unwanted, and that in most individuals cause marked anxiety or distress. The individual attempts to ignore or suppress such thoughts, urges, or images, or to neutralize them with some thought or action (i.e., by performing a compulsion). The obsessions or compulsions are time consuming (e.g., take more than 1 hour per day) or cause clinically significant distress or impairment in social, occupational, or other important areas of functioning.

I like to think of these intrusive thoughts as an unpleasant song (think of an annoying kids' song or a game show theme) that plays on an endless loop, over and over, louder and louder, until the entire day is consumed by it and leaves you believing this thought will become a reality. For some it can manifest as the fear of losing a job, for others it could be the fear of catching a serious illness. For me it manifested as terrifying thoughts of harming others, both strangers and loved ones alike.

My OCD in Action

Growing up, I felt anxious all the time and I knew I had OCD from around the age of 7, but it had not been diagnosed. I couldn't turn my brain off, that bright shiny object spinning around like a disco ball in my head shouting "look at me, look at me," despite trying as hard as I could to push those thoughts away. I relied on checking rituals, like turning the light switch on and off, pulling and tugging on every door handle—everything done three times exactly lest something terrible happen to me or someone I loved.

I had sleeping issues, which included the fear of going to sleep and not being able to fall asleep. I listened to my AM/FM radio in bed each night like a security blanket. I used to think obsessively throughout the day about the night to come. I'd be in school obsessing about the fact that I wasn't going to be able to sleep that night, sometimes walking in the hallways from classroom to classroom, fearful that the day was inching closer to evening. Trepidation in its purest form.

I'd obsess all day about the night to come.

I constantly acted out in self-destructive ways. This included acting out in class, blaming others for my own perceived shortcomings, and publicly taunting and berating not only my athletic competitors but also my teammates, eventually leading my high school friends to nickname me "ego man." I was further horrified when one of my teachers began calling me by that name. What appeared funny to the outside world carried with it a deep sense of shame and embarrassment to this teenage kid.

Each morning I awoke feeling what I can only describe as a "bubbling cauldron of dread" paired with an inescapable sense of impending doom. You see, I was also struggling through undiagnosed Post-Traumatic Stress Disorder (PTSD), which, left to its own devices, can and will fester like an open wound while presenting in many ways, living each day in fight or flight mode, unaware that thoughts and actions are simply reactions formed long ago during childhood years. In many cases, yours truly included, we spend our lives waging a silent battle against the symptoms without ever stopping, if even for a moment, to realize there is a suppressed trauma or traumas hidden at its core.

> *Each morning I awoke feeling a "bubbling cauldron of dread."*

A Pivotal Moment

To make this more relatable, allow me to be vulnerable and share the life-altering event that finally led me to tell someone. Unlike the panic attacks, sleepless nights, and intrusive thoughts of years past, this time was different. So different, in fact, I can say with certainty, that the trajectory of my journey changed forever during the late summer of 2004.

Between jobs, I had just returned home to New York City from a trip to Jacksonville, Florida, where I spent time assisting a colleague with financial analysis work. On flights to and from Jacksonville, I was engrossed in Robert Ludlum's best-selling thriller *The Bourne Identity*, where the main character suffers retrograde amnesia and seeks to regain his identity. This book and its underlying theme would soon play a key role in the events that follow.

During that trip, I accepted a new and exciting finance role with the Treasury group at a large consumer products company. I had spent the prior few weeks interviewing, eagerly awaiting an offer. It was the first time in my career where I could step away from the extremely high stress, fast-paced Wall Street life, a major transition I had been looking forward to yet struggling with for months.

Upon returning home, I could feel that something was a bit off. The vise that would often squeeze my temples and surround the back of my head returned without invitation, as it so often did during times of rising stress. As usual, I ignored the physical symptoms, attributing them to my recent travel and hoping they would dissipate with a good night's sleep. Once again, a major physical red flag got missed.

August 24th and the start of my new job brought with it all the emotions and questions of the first day of school. *Will they like me? What will my new colleagues be like? What exactly will I be doing?* But one overriding thought trumped them all... *Will they find out that I really don't know what I'm doing?* Cue my lifelong sidekick, an extension of my anxiety, Imposter Syndrome, except back then I had no idea what it was nor that so many others shared a similar misguided worry about being a fraud or not the person they claimed to be. I just kept thinking, "When are they going to find me out?"

Twenty-eight floors up in a midtown Manhattan office building next to the famed Ziegfield Theater, my first couple of weeks began like I imagined they did for everyone else—corporate onboarding, introduction to a whole new group of people, and the introduction to my new cubicle where I would once again be reconnected with my old friend and sometimes nemesis, Microsoft Excel. And, oh yeah, the deepening of my Imposter Syndrome.

As the first two weeks continued, symptoms of anxiety and stress began to overtake my body. The vise-like headaches consumed my waking hours. I lost my ability to concentrate, often watching colleagues move their lips in conversation but not really hearing or processing their words. Alongside me, like an unwanted friend, was the irrational internal voice questioning, "Can they see through my façade, and, if so, how much longer before I'm found out and they fire me?"

"How much longer before they fire me?"

Why I Missed the Signs

At this point you might wonder why I didn't see this coming. After a lifetime spent dealing with anxiety and OCD, how could any of this possibly be a surprise anymore? Yet throughout my life, I somehow never saw these warning signs.

Was it denial? No, I really don't think it was. I never found myself saying internally, "This isn't happening to you." In fact, my internal dialogue during all those years had been the complete opposite. It often started with the exact same words: "I can't believe this is happening again" and typically ended with "I'm not sure if I can go through this again." Looking back, what I truly thought each time was that it wouldn't possibly be as bad or scary as all those other times. *There is no way that could possibly happen.* After all, I was at a company I quickly came to love in a role that promised to utilize all the skills I'd honed the first eleven years of my Wall Street career... and I was "happy."

Everyone thought I was living a "normal" and "successful" life, including me. I was gainfully employed, successful in many prior roles, had recently earned a master's degree in finance, and was set to put it to work in a new capacity. I wore the pin-striped suits, fancy Hermès ties, and even had the Rolex watch adorning my wrist. The cold reality was I wasn't thriving. I was being the person I thought everyone else wanted me to be—just another manifestation of the façade I had been wearing since childhood.

I spent my entire life in a silent battle with Harm OCD.

Remember my mention of *The Bourne Identity*? To show how quickly OCD can manifest itself, I sat in our apartment toward the end of the second week and, while mindlessly watching television, I began mentally quizzing myself out of a growing fear that I was losing my memory. I had spent my life in a silent battle with Harm OCD, but now I was confronted by a whole new animal that had popped its head out of the jungle and was ready to pounce on my fear and insecurity.

Seemingly out of nowhere, I entered the realm of Memory Hoarding which, for me, primarily centered around sports events and figures, movies and actors and attempting to remember dates that meaningful sporting events happened. I specifically remember watching a Red Sox game while at the same time reciting each of the players, their respective field positions and spots in the batting order on the 1986 World Series roster, each time internally berating myself and growing increasingly more frustrated when my memory "failed" me. I had somehow transferred the issues of the book's main character onto myself and had no idea at the time that this was a manifestation of OCD.

> *I entered the realm of Memory Hording.*

Late on that Friday afternoon, my wife Amy and I left for a pre-planned weekend visit to her dad's house in Albany, New York. All weekend my sleeping pattens were interrupted, and eating came in fits and starts as my appetite drifted into the abyss, while my levels of agitation and irritability crept higher and higher. There was even a round of Saturday golf spent frustrated at almost every shot with an overwhelming desire to leave the course and return to a more safe and secure location. All the while, I continued with my mysterious memory games, all aimed at making me feel safer about my situation but leaving me mentally exhausted and barely able to remember my own birthday. Once again, a series of bright red flashing warning lights should have been dancing across my vision but once again I raced right past with reckless abandon.

Sunday afternoon arrived and, to the best of my recollection, we said our pleasant goodbyes and loaded the car for the two-hour drive home to New York City. As we pulled away from her dad's house, I drove in the direction of the New York State Thruway, a trip I had completed dozens of times before, to the point where I could have driven it blindfolded—or so I thought.

Not long after entering the Thruway, I began to experience a strange tunnel vision. I soon found myself staring out onto the highway as though looking through two drinking straws. Panic mounted and I started to forget where I was. A few moments later I didn't even realize I was driving. Scarier still was the fact I had been having a conversation with Amy that I didn't even realize was taking place.

Sheer terror settled in while one thought overwhelmed my brain: *What is happening to me?*

Not knowing what else to do and fearing for our safety, with every bit of energy I had remaining, I finally said to Amy, "I need to pull over the car now. Something is very wrong with me, but I don't know what it is."

Panic mounted and I started to forget where I was.

The last thing I remember before my world went completely black was sitting in the passenger seat of our rental car, tears streaming down my face, weeping uncontrollably that I missed my friends. These were emotions that I felt so strongly, and yet I couldn't place why they had sprung up just then. As someone who was raised not to share emotions, I had not shed tears about anything in decades.

Was this, for perhaps the very first time in my adult life, my inner child, who I have subsequently named "Little Erik," presenting himself to the outside world? Was it also no coincidence that I longed for friends at what would have been the start of a school year? Whatever the reason, it set off a series of emotions so deep that I can only compare it to the overwhelming grief we feel for the loss of a loved one. And then, without any warning, the world went completely dark and all recollection of time and space was lost. So dark, in fact, that I heard no sounds, felt no emotions, nor saw anything out the front windshield for the remaining ninety minutes of the drive.

When I started to recognize reality again, Amy had successfully navigated us to New York City where we returned the rental car and took a short walk to a familiar neighborhood diner. A wave of euphoria overtook me and the feelings of fear and dread that had anchored themselves in my stomach were replaced by a food craving so ferocious one would have thought I was a castaway rescued from months of isolation on a deserted island. All I could think about was how deeply I wanted breakfast for dinner, one of life's greatest guilty pleasures.

As I sat at the table frantically stuffing my face full of eggs, corned beef hash, and French fries, my euphoria built to a crescendo, resulting in a soliloquy of stream of consciousness thoughts, gushing forth from my lips like water from a firehouse at a five-alarm blaze. Not a word of it do I remember, however the albatross that had draped my shoulders for days suddenly flew away, leaving me to think, *This is it! This is really it! I feel so ecstatic because, for the first time in my life, I am finally cured of the terrible nightmare that had been my constant companion for decades.* Oh, I was so terribly wrong.

Now It Was Time to Tell Someone!

Upon returning to our apartment, which was only a short walk from the diner, I sat at my desk and attempted to collect myself. The euphoria wore off and I was desperately in need of answers regarding what had just happened. As I tried to explain it to Amy, I thought of our next-door neighbor, who was a close friend and also a psychiatrist. To be clear, I still did not think I was in need of therapy. Rather, I thought she might be able to explain what had happened to me during that drive home.

The neighbor listened intently as I recounted not only the car ride home from Albany, but also the physical and mental experiences of the preceding weeks. When she finally spoke, her words came to me in a calm and soothing manner with an explanation I could fully understand. She likened it to doing a reboot on a computer where my brain had been so overwhelmed for such a long period of time that it shut itself down temporarily so I would prevent myself from doing any further damage. In other words, my amygdala—the primitive part of the brain's decision-making process and a major processing center for emotions, which for decades had been my CEO and decision maker rather than my prefrontal cortex—had reached a level of extreme danger. It shut itself down, in the same way a nuclear reactor shuts down to prevent a meltdown, to prevent the mind and body from becoming its own Chernobyl.

After a somewhat restful night's sleep, I returned to work the next day, the euphoria of the prior evening replaced by that familiar sense of impending doom. Within a few days, the downward spiral took hold again and I found it difficult to focus on work. Even the very act of getting out of bed became agonizing and terrifying. On a couple of occasions, I found myself in the bathroom stall at work quietly crying and wondering how I was going to make it through the day. At some point that week, with strong encouragement from Amy and my last remaining energy, I decided for the first time to speak to a therapist. It was time to tell someone.

At age 33 and fresh off the throes of my first dissociative episode—defined by the Mayo Clinic as mental disorders that involve experiencing a disconnection and lack of continuity between thoughts, memories, surroundings, actions and identity—I finally went to a therapist and started unraveling all these complicated things because I couldn't take it anymore and I wanted to live a better life.

Amy took me to see her therapist for an evaluation and joined me in a joint session. I remember two vivid moments from that visit. The first was when her therapist looked at the two of us and said, "You two are extremely lucky to have found each other." The second is when she said I would be just fine and referred me to my own therapist, and one of the most amazing people to have ever come into my life, Dr. K.

With the help of my adoring wife and treasured therapist Dr. K, I finally began to find my voice. What I could not have possibly known at the time was that the voice I found was so loud and powerful, that it led me to recognize my heart, own my feelings and truly take care of myself. I was finally diagnosed with General Anxiety Disorder and OCD and, along with weekly therapy sessions, I was prescribed Prozac, a drug I take to this day to help ease my racing mind. The memory of those early morning sessions with Dr. K, who has since passed on after a life filled with great care and service to others, brings a smile to my face as his kind and gentle demeanor never wavered, even when faced with a spiraling NYC finance executive.

> With help, I finally began to find my voice.

I resigned from my 18-year corporate career in September 2011 to move west. My wife, two cats, and I headed to the snow-capped mountains of Colorado where my full healing process could finally unfold and where, in January 2021, I founded the mental health podcast *From Survivor to Thriver*. I started to share my story, person by person, each time growing a bit stronger. These days my *why* is focused on helping create a world where people can speak openly and honestly about their mental health issues without fear of judgment as I once did.

For a long time I hid my daily battles well. I wasn't "okay," "good," or "fine." I was struggling. Sometimes a little and other times a lot, but always in silence. I *never* let anyone know. At the time, I thought I'd never share the details of my journey so openly with family, let alone in a book. As I look back now, it didn't have to be that way for me. And it certainly doesn't have to be that way for you!

Reflecting on the early parts of my life, it is fair to say that I spent it running *from* something. Sometimes running so fast and furious my brain could no longer keep pace and shut itself down for my own safety and well-being. It was only after telling someone that I was able to change the narrative and, for the very first time, run *to* something.

I write this as both a reminder and a plea for all of us to recognize that there is no stigma in experiencing trauma, depression, or anxiety, and in allowing those emotions to flow freely. Mental illness can impact anyone at any time. In no way does it discriminate due to one's socioeconomic status or physical strength and vitality. As a long-time sufferer of OCD and anxiety, I know all too well how repressed feelings can suddenly, and often at the most inconvenient times, burst to the surface like a tsunami with nary a care for what or who is directly in its path.

> *There is no shame in experiencing trauma, depression, or anxiety.*

It is with this in mind that I ask you to become your own advocate. Reach out to someone you trust who you know will not pass judgment: friends, family, loved ones, or licensed mental health professionals, to talk about how you're feeling in the face of uncertainty. Just as we attend annual physicals with a primary care physician, so too should we attend mental health "check-ups" with licensed professionals. Caring for our mental health is not a "one and done" process, but, rather, part of a larger wellness journey. Please, take the time to be introspective as you, too, may have pushed on in the face of uncertain times and, consciously or not, didn't hit the pause button to address what you were truly feeling.

Stigma says we shouldn't talk openly about these things. I say we should! Stigma also says we shouldn't stand high upon the mountain top, vulnerable and transparent, for the entire world to see. I say we must! Today, after many years of therapy in different phases of my post-2004 life, I still live with PTSD (diagnosed in November 2021), anxiety, and OCD. The difference is it no longer manages me nor defines who I am. I keep the overwhelming parts at bay and use aspects of those things to my advantage, almost like superpowers. These days when people ask how I am, I like to answer with, "Thank you so much for asking. I am a much better version of my former self."

As my friend on the U.S. Ski Team, Tess Johnson, likes to say, "It's cool to be vulnerable." I take it one step further... because I want it to be 100 percent clear that being vulnerable isn't a weakness. Talking about how you're feeling is a sign of strength. Being vulnerable is a superpower. Being vulnerable and staring those challenging times in the face allows you to do hard things. And telling someone about your struggles is, for a fact, one of those hard things. You have such a powerful and impactful voice!

Mental illness can impact anyone at any time.

As the signs plastered inside all the NYC subway cars state, "If you see something, say something." I have changed just one word of that famous saying to fit the mental health narrative, "If you *feel* something, say something." Together, let's work to break the stigma of mental illness and remind one another that it's perfectly okay to not always be okay.

Remember, you're not alone in your journey. We're all in this together. There is HOPE, there is HELP and there IS a way through. We all deserve to experience as much joy in our lives as is humanly possible. Collectively, with a bit of patience and a willingness to tell someone, we'll get through this. I promise.

Erik DaRosa

ERIK DaROSA, known by friends as "Yoda," is the Founder and CEO of From Survivor to Thriver, a mental health advocate, speaker, author and Co-host of the popular *From Survivor to Thriver* podcast. Through his work and his own lived experience, Erik is upending the front-end of the mental health space and building a bridge between those who seek resources and those who provide both help and hope. Each week on his podcast, he tackles different mental health topics through honest and relatable "kitchen table" conversations with real people who are helping to shatter mental health stigmas and find their voices. He aims to normalize discussions around mental health topics and remind his audience they are not alone, there is strength in community, and "it's perfectly okay to not always be okay."

Born and raised in New England, Erik earned his MBA from the NYU Stern School of Business and his BA in Economics from Brandeis University. He lives in Colorado with his wife Amy and two cats, Lincoln and Taylor.

www.fromsurvivortothriver.com

Feeling the Fear and Doing It Anyway

Corrine Statia Thomas

IT WAS THE DAY BEFORE MY BIRTHDAY, March 23, 2020, and I watched the news, which I had been glued to for weeks, filled with anxiety as Naval hospital ships were being sent to New York and California to support the Coronavirus response. Individual states had imposed "stay-at-home" orders to stop the spread of the virus. Our lives were turned upside down, and on that day I received a special gift—my left arm was stuck to my side.

To stop the excruciating torment, I put not one, not two, but three lidocaine patches on my upper arm and shoulder. It gave very little relief. The pain was relentless. Television provided enough distraction to stop me from wanting to chop off the left side of my body.

That night I passed out for the first time. I thought it was the end. My husband called 911. When I woke, even though I was in so much pain and distress, I refused to go to the hospital. During the quarantine, so many who entered a hospital never came home.

It turns out that I had put on too many lidocaine patches. After that incident, out of fear, I turned to Excedrin instead. The pain was unbearable. Desperate for relief, I again took more than I should have. Sure enough, a couple days later I passed out. My husband had to call 911 again. This time the EMTs said I was dehydrated.

I made a point of drinking more water and used muscle relaxers to help manage the pain. I got used to living without the use of my left arm until June when doctors began using telemedicine—essentially a doctor's visit via video—because we were still all on lockdown due to the pandemic.

During the appointment, I described what had transpired since March. My doctor was awestruck by how I had dealt with my plight, but understood my concern about not going to the hospital. She was very disturbed by how I looked though. She kept saying, "You look so twisted! I'm very concerned." I was really a hot mess, but had gotten used to the pain.

She prescribed an anti-inflammatory and referred me to an orthopedic specialist. Thanks to the medicine, I felt some pain relief for the first time in months. I was able to get an appointment with the orthopedic doctor within a week. Yes, I went out to a medical facility—not a hospital—and had my left side examined and x-rayed.

After meeting with the specialist, he explained that I had a frozen shoulder, which would require physical therapy. I had never heard of such a thing. As I understood it, the cushiony material in my shoulder socket had thickened and inflamed. My shoulder could no longer move, ergo a frozen shoulder.

The specialist reassured me that I would regain the use of my arm and shoulder again. However, when I asked how this had happened in the first place, he said I was just unlucky. He prescribed strong ibuprofen and an anti-inflammatory which helped with the pain tremendously.

After four months of twice-weekly therapy, I regained full use of my left arm and shoulder. Shout out to physical therapists—they are amazingly good at what they do. I learned that others faced the same issue during this time. They started calling it "Covid-Shoulder," related to stress and working at a desktop computer for extended periods. This made sense to me because I worked at my computer a whole heck of a lot, and I seemed to be addicted to work.

> *I learned that others faced the same issue... they called it "Covid-Shoulder."*

Grateful for regaining the use of my arm and shoulder, I knew I had faced my fear—leaving the house and entering a medical facility—and done what was needed.

Before 2020, I thought everything was going quite well. It had been about 14 years since I'd left my "corporate situation" to start my own business—Absolute Events By Corrine. It was gutsy, but I made it a success.

I had grown settled in my world of meeting and conference planning, peppered with special events here and there... like fundraising galas that are a joy to plan and execute.

I work with clients to determine their event budget and dates, which helps decide on appropriate venues and determine the number of attendees. Sometimes an otherwise perfect venue doesn't have enough hotel guest rooms. Other times a venue has ample guest rooms but not enough meeting space. Yet other times, the meeting space is already booked for another group on the same dates. It is a dance to find a happy medium, or to get creative.

Everything relies first on having a venue and a date, as contracts for all other services revolve around those first details. A site visit is also required to ensure nothing would have a negative impact on the event. For example, a venue needs to be ADA-compliant since some guests may need a wheelchair ramp or elevator. I once made an impromptu site visit, only to find major construction in the lobby. Hotel staff had neglected to inform me. Even though I had my heart set on that being the perfect venue, we had to go back to the drawing board.

There are many challenges of meeting planning that most people don't see or even think about. Nor should they. When the job is done well, it appears effortless. That is both a blessing and a curse. When a magician makes a trick look too easy, no one appreciates the amount of work and practice required to make the experience "magical."

It was gutsy to start my own business. But I faced the fear and did it anyway, making something from nothing and succeeding for 18 years. That was before the pandemic struck. In 2020, live events came to a screeching halt because of the Covid-19 lockdown.

The meeting and event industry spiraled downwards. I count myself fortunate that one of my clients decided to turn their spring 2020 conference into a virtual event, even before the lockdown was announced. That event was very successful, so I continued planning virtual meetings and conferences during the rest of 2020 well into 2021.

For two years, I had a lot of time to think about what my corporate and entrepreneurial life had been like. It occurred to me that I had amassed a great deal of information, wisdom, and a broad range of

I faced the fear and did it anyway.

experiences. I kept having this feeling that I should do something meaningful with these experiences and the pearls of wisdom I had gathered along the way.

But in stepping out to share my experiences and knowledge to help others, I found myself fighting imposter syndrome. Each day, I asked myself, "What makes you think that what you have to share would be of use to anyone?" I experienced a mix of self-doubt and excitement as I began creating a second new business.

While it can be difficult to trust my own strengths and knowledge, a strong desire to help others improve and work toward their professional goals drives me. Whether or not this business venture will be successful, I'm looking forward to getting started and having the chance to take my skills and experience as an entrepreneur to the next level.

Yes, it seems a little crazy to start a new business while I'm still running another one. If I'm honest, it's a little scary as well. But I have been in this situation before and learned a lot in the process.

I use the fear as fuel to propel me forward.

One powerful technique I learned is to write down my "whys." Initially, I brushed off this advice because it made no sense to me. My "why" was already in my head; I didn't need to write it down. It took years for me to realize that the mere act of writing forced me to hold myself to a higher standard, and to find ways of getting there.

Try that tool for yourself because it is amazingly powerful.

Whatever your desire, whether it means moving your business or your life forward to the next level, if it scares you, just go ahead and be scared... and do it anyway. Ask yourself, "What do I have to lose?" Then write down your "why" every day. I promise this will keep you motivated.

Thank you for letting me share my thoughts and fears with you and for reading this chapter. Now, go be the best that you can be!

CORRINE STATIA THOMAS

After relocating to the United States from England, CORRINE STATIA THOMAS became a Corporate Executive with two well-known corporations. In one of those roles, Corrine worked with a team that helped manage, plan, and execute more than 500 meetings, conferences, and special events in a little over one year. Since then, her company has helped organize Corporate Events for KPMG, BD, Novartis, Financial Planning Association of New Jersey, Maersk Sealand, Victoria Secret Beauty, Time Warner Cable, National Hispanic Business Group, NJEDge.Net, Blue Vine, Christian Dior, and a host of others.

Corrine owns and operates a Full-Service Meeting and Event Planning company that organizes and plans all aspects of meetings and events. It provides management and logistic services to corporations, associations, non-profit organizations, consumers, and more. The company's mission is to create successful and memorable experiences for its clients that enable them to be guests at their events.

Corrine has over 20 years of event industry experience producing corporate events that range from training meetings, conferences, business marketing cocktail receptions, employee recognition events, company picnics or outings, fundraising galas, meetings, and conferences as well as social events that range from cocktail receptions and milestone events to leadership retreats and team building.

Prior to this, Corrine served in various IT roles that included Systems Analysis and Technical Support. She now brings her IT experience to bear through building efficiency into the planning and production services and is quickly able to determine the best tools to use in particular situations.

Corrine has felt called to share her knowledge and experiences by creating a business growth program to empower and build up small business owners to become 'Founders' who create the impact they were created for.

Corrine Statia Thomas CMP

Founder, Meetings & Events Specialist

Absolute Events by Corrine

www.absoluteeventsbycorrine.com

cs@absoluteeventsbycorrine.com

For more information on the
Business Growth Program, visit:

https://virtualevents.mykajabi.com/CBGB?preview_theme_id=2153069915

Blessings Within a Moment

Deb Weilnau

OPPORTUNITIES SURROUND US EACH AND EVERY DAY... decisions that ask us to step out of our comfort zone. Moments that ask us if we are willing to face our F.E.A.R.—Face Everything And Rise, or Forget Everything And Run. Times filled with discomfort, unknowns that may require us to change, stretching us in ways we never would have imagined.

Even though not all risks come with rewards, they grant us experiences that contain a wide range of perspectives. Some come as lessons that need to be learned, and they keep coming back around, again and again, until we finally decide to open our eyes, our hearts, and our minds. For me, until something hits my doorstep or affects someone within my inner circle, I usually don't exert energy to help alleviate the situation. It's easier to stay on the fringe, on the outside looking in, judging and even spewing unsolicited advice without knowing what the other person is going through.

We listen to respond, but we tend to avoid listening to understand. We let our emotions run wild, expounding on things we have not experienced, because we believe we can do it better. How often have you heard someone say they would not allow themselves to become a battered woman? She would not fall into the trap of a narcissist. How many times have you had conversations with friends who have no children, yet know how to handle parenting situations better than those who do have children?

I never thought in a million years that I would ever allow myself to enter into or remain in a long-term verbally abusive relationship... and yet I did. I became unrecognizable. Mentally and physically, I was a mess. I remember the day she kicked me out. I was still begging my abuser to stay, touting that I would change, I would bend, I would, I would, I would... What I didn't realize was that her selfishness and infatuation with her new muse gave me the greatest gifts of all.

Jane wanted me out of the house, so she pushed me to obtain my undergraduate degree in Business Administration, while she secured her newest prize. She told me I didn't make enough money and that I brought little value to our relationship, when in actuality, I was carrying 90 percent of the load. She then complained that we were together too much. It was a winning proposition for her. She would know where I was and who I was with, and she could play as much as she desired. Her selfishness actually gave me the opportunity to get my degree and earn the pay increase I would need to support myself.

> *I was still begging my abuser to stay.*

During the last semester of my senior year, I was working with a group to prepare and present our capstone project. Jane began to make insinuating remarks to family and friends that I was cheating on her with someone from my class, this way I would be the "Reason Why." In hindsight, the day our relationship ended was the greatest gift anyone has ever given me.

At the time, I didn't understand it as a great gift though. You see, narcissists only release their victims when they have a replacement. Narcissists do not like to be held accountable for their actions, so they devise ways to blame their victims.

The psychological damage from that six-year relationship taught me more than I ever thought I would learn. I now understand why women beg to stay in abusive situations, and why they are always looking over their shoulders for their abusers.

Jane and I worked for the same company. Though she was stationed in a different plant, that did not stop her from trying to regain control after she discovered her new muse was not as vulnerable as she once thought.

My head was such a mess, I trembled anytime she was near. She intentionally came and sat a few cubicle rows away from me.

Though I couldn't see her, I could hear her voice. My nerves were shot, and I began to shake, but there was nowhere to hide.

I went to therapy weekly, sometimes bi-weekly, to try to overcome the abuse I'd endured. As I write this, I am realizing that the rise and fall of this abusive relationship gave me a detour from my path, and a lesson that propelled me to achieve so much more than I could have foreseen.

Jane was always looking for ways to blame me for why the relationship was ending. She even told me that I needed to go to counseling because I was crazy. I was the problem. I remember sitting in the therapist's office. The therapist asked each of us to say what we loved about the other. I responded with a list of reasons, while Jane responded, "I have nothing." At the time, I was extremely codependent—exactly where she wanted me to be. In this realm, I was her victim. I wouldn't fight back or ever gain enough confidence to leave, like a fly within the spider's web.

When Jane decided to use my therapist against me, she led me to the one person who could help me most—the woman who has been my guardian angel ever since I was 21 years old. For decades, I lied to my therapist, to family, and to friends, but most of all, I lied to myself. This time, I truly hit my bottom. At age 42, I had to move in with my parents. I was financially buried and psychologically reduced to rubble. This time I got honest with my therapist. Guess what... I started to get stronger and healthier.

> *I lied to my therapist, to family, and to friends...*

It took several years to overcome the fear of Jane's voice or of running into her somewhere. As I gained confidence, I went back to college to obtain a Master's in Business Administration. This really helped me fill time in a positive, healthy, and safe environment. At the end of the first semester, my higher power blessed me yet again in a way I could not yet see—I was one of 500 workers laid off. The factory where Jane and I worked, a company I planned to retire from, a company with which I had just gained tenure... it had been the place of my longest employment.

Getting laid off was traumatic, but it was exactly what I needed to remove Jane from my life. Once she no longer had access to me, I could finally heal without slipping back into old patterns or reliving the trauma. It also forced me out of my comfort zone, and opened the door for me to realize my worth. I had been stagnating and would never have reached the level of promotion there that I deserved.

It also gave me time to finish the accelerated MBA program with less stress. The program consisted of four-hour classes, four days per week. At the time, I was driving an hour and a half to campus, which made for long days while working the factory job.

People tend to think that getting laid off is like a vacation, but they are unable to identify with the disappointment, struggle, hardship, and heartbreak that comes with it. Plus unemployment does not pay as much as your job; it's a stipend that barely covers the necessities. Due to the costs of Cobra or independent health insurance, there is also often nothing to help in the case of emergency or illness.

Mentally, I struggled after losing my job. I couldn't think straight and had a difficult time learning. My mind was always focused on finding a new job. I remember walking into my communication's professor's office, sharing with her that I was thinking about dropping out of the program due to mental and financial issues. She looked at me and said, "Keep going at all costs. See it through. If you don't, you will regret it." She went on to tell me, "You can do this. Things are hard right now but you will find a job and get back on your feet again. Just don't give up."

> *I was thinking about dropping out.*

Yet again, someone had been placed in my life to keep me on the path to finding my life's purpose. Because that professor took the time out of her day to have that discussion, I was prepared for what was soon to come.

The last two semesters were hard, I was still living with my parents and receiving a constant flow of rejections to job applications. I was beginning to lose hope that things were ever going to get any better.

Then it happened. I received a job offer to be a Quality Manager, earning more money than ever before, starting the day after the graduation procession for my MBA.

Things started to turn around; it wasn't long before I was able to purchase a house. For the first time ever, I was living by myself, which was scary. I had no one to count on if anything happened, but I used the money-managing skills I learned while being jobless.

Then I started a job in an unfamiliar field, entered a PhD program beyond my level of competence, and began teaching as an adjunct professor at a local university. What could possibly go wrong?

Hired to replace a woman who was retiring, I was supposed to shadow her for six months to learn the position. The company was also supposed to send me for certification training to learn the ins and outs of FDA rules, regulations, and requirements. But the retiree could not give up control, which made it nearly impossible to learn the position. I spoke with the Director of Quality, who requested that I fly to California so he could help get me up to speed with their processes. When I arrived at the plant, he told me he would introduce me to the team an hour later. Instead he announced that he was leaving the organization. When we were later alone, I asked if I should start looking for another job—because it's common for a new director to bring their own staff, which meant my days would be numbered. It took a total of nine months for the company and I to part ways, which eventually came as a huge relief. This position was not a good fit.

Unemployed again, at least I had part-time income from adjunct teaching. The university offered me two additional classes, which really helped. Teaching gave me presence. It allowed an opportunity to work through my fear of public speaking. It also opened my eyes to another passion—I quickly realized that I teach and am willing to be taught... everywhere I go.

Then the skies opened up...

For the first time in my life, I felt decent about my financial situation. Then the skies opened up again and my higher power reintroduced me to my marketing professor—a woman who had seen me as a shell of a person in an abusive relationship. She asked me to come to Florida to spend a week with her and her husband. At first, I declined. It was way out of my comfort zone. We spoke on the phone for hours one night and she helped me book the flight.

I was nervous about maneuvering airports, staying at someone's house, and spending the money. Old frugal patterns are hard to break. But she was there for me, teaching me how to travel, acclimating me to different airports and showing me that I am strong enough to do things on my own. Sure, it's all scary at first, then it turns into something magical—an adventure!

If someone would have told me that one trip would lead me to my life's purpose, I would not have believed them, but it's true. She gave me an assignment, an important one. Kevin Hines was speaking at my university. He had attempted suicide and lived to talk about how it changed his life. Again, right place, right time. I stood in the back of the room, guarded. Yet, at that moment, it hit me. My story had value, and like Kevin, I could speak to others to help save lives. It's funny how things work out, if only we are willing to step out of our comfort zone long enough to gain a glimpse of what's possible.

One trip led me to my life's purpose.

Just like the job situation, the Ph.D. program in which I was enrolled was not a good fit. I was placed on academic probation, which led me to the Quality Systems Certificate program to regain my academic standing, which became a segue into being accepted into the Doctorate of Organizational Development and Change program.

I was accepted but the very first meeting turned me off. I realized that I did not mesh with my cohort group, but kept going until I became unemployed. Again, my higher power had a plan. This blockage needed to happen for me to be at the right place at the right time. A year passed and now I'm working with a different cohort, a group of individuals that matches my insight.

This is where I met Robyn. We became instantaneous friends. She in turn introduced me to the founder of Scars to Stars, Deana Brown Mitchell. I attended her summit and realized that my story had value, and that I too could share my story to help others, especially after the seed planted by my marketing professor. In that moment, I knew I wanted to speak at Deana's next summit. I too wanted to share my story, a test to see if others found value from what I had to say.

Deana formulated this series for authors to come together, each with different experience and perspectives, to share the trials and tribulations that had held us back from becoming the best versions of themselves—moments that help those who are still struggling to realize they are not alone... we all struggle.

In those dark moments that lead to the light, to the jelly in the jellyroll, that's usually where we find our life's purpose. The most precious moments are when you can look at your life and see the disguised "blessings" that led you to your path. When things don't work out the way we want them to, it often leads us to things we don't believe that we deserve. Once you see the pattern clearly, life changes. You give up trying to control everything and can just live in the moment, where we all belong, which is the only moment we can influence.

Robyn influenced my life in so many ways and yet she was not done. The DODC program was not a good fit for either of us. She tried to get me to transfer to a program in the UK, one that would be exactly what both of us were looking for, one that plays to my strengths, my passions, and my experience. That program is allowing me to write my master's thesis on finding my voice. You see, we all have a purpose. We all add value to others' lives, even if it's something simple like saying, "Good morning," to someone you pass on the street. People are blessings and you are too.

The puzzle that is my life began to take shape.

I challenge you to look at your life as if it were a jigsaw puzzle. As you begin to see the image come into focus, can you spot the people or obstacles placed in your path, those things that irritated you and yet later on, you were glad they turned out differently? Can you see the chain reaction of events that led to where you are today? Are they blessings? Indeed they are, even if you can't see that immediately.

The puzzle that is my life began to take shape only after I became frustrated and overwhelmed. Before that, all I chose to see was a jumble of pieces dumped out of a box. I could not recognize the small wins that would become the border pieces, the foundation of a beautiful life that was meant for me. Instead, I was always sorting, frantically trying to put random pieces together to secure some semblance of peace. Little did I realize, the pieces were coming together behind the scenes. With every job loss or bad decision, I was "picking up the pieces," finding corner pieces that helped me to anchor this journey that is my life. Every time I exuded vulnerability and became willing to grow and learn from those trials and tribulations, my higher power blessed me with another chunk of the border. Little by little, as the frame began to develop, my confidence grew until I finally allowed myself to see the beauty that is life.

For so many years, I searched through the pile for that one puzzle piece that would make me whole—thinking it was another person—a piece I recently discovered is not included in my puzzle for a good reason. My path is for me to become the best version of myself. It's a path I was meant to walk alone, but it is graciously filled with individuals who have guided me along the way. I see life differently now; I realize I don't need a partner to fulfill me or to make me happy. I desire a partner who is her own person. Together, we can be two strong independent women who are great apart but even better together. Now, I am no longer searching frantically for a jigsaw person to complete me. My focus is on how I can share my own story and lessons learned.

> *I realize I don't need a partner to fulfill me or make me happy.*

All of the pieces are already in front of us—pieces piled in disarray, maybe, but they are all there. Don't worry or fret. Some pieces are topsy turvy, upside down, or even sideways. Live in this very moment. Stop trying to jam the pieces into place, attempting to control everything. Instead, be willing to learn. Listen and look past the obvious to see the blessings your life is offering.

We all face struggles and have had to "pick up the pieces," so to speak. What I've learned is simple but not easy. Lead with compassion and understanding, then share your own story and treat others as you wish to be treated. Life is hard and everyone is not where you are. Some are more advanced, while others are still searching for a border or corner piece. Wherever you are in your own struggles, remember also that you might just be the missing piece someone else desperately needs so they can begin to build the frame for their own life.

DEB WEILNAU

DEBORAH S. WEILNAU is a Quality Manager who also enjoys her role as an Adjunct Professor in her spare time. She specializes in teaching Supply Chain Management, Materials Management, and Quality Management. Growing up in a family-owned business, she was able to witness firsthand the successful operations of a company through fluctuating economies. Early exposure to a business environment has made her an authentic individual who desires to help businesses communicate effectively.

Deb received her B.S. in Business Administration and her MBA from Heidelberg University. She is currently working on a M.S. in the Transdisciplinary Practitioner programme at Middlesex University in the UK. She continues to search for the right program as to obtain her Ph.D. so she can create a consulting business that will help develop businesses.

Unfortunate crucible moments that have occurred during her career have enabled her to gain immense perspective on business operations. Adopting fear and change as a motivator, her aggressive, tenacious, altruistic, and transparent management style drives the necessary movements for organizational development.

Her personal agenda is to become the best version of herself. She empowers and promotes others in a fashion that increases morale and fosters an environment based upon learning.

If one sentence was used to define her it would be "Any day that I think I am better than I am, is the day that my higher power reminds me I still have much to learn."

www.linkedin.com/in/deborah-weilnau-mba-88242a97

"I Ain't Goin' Nowhere!"

Marcia Dixon

It was 2006 when we received a knock at our door. There stood the mother of one of our traveling basketball team players. Her family had come upon hard times and asked if she and her five children could park their vehicle at the edge of our yard and stay there until she could find another place to live. Feeling her pain, we said, "What! Stay in your car, no way. You all can stay in our home while you are seeking other living accommodations. However, we're sorry that all we have to offer you all are blankets and pillows for sleeping in our family room." She was very thankful and agreed to stay with us.

Months passed by and our guests were still living in our home. It was bittersweet as a few of the kids had behavioral issues and other problems that kept us, especially my husband, busy assisting the mother with doctors' appointments and designing ways to help her kids stay on track with school and sports. This caused a lot of overwhelm for our family as we were raising our own five children, with our middle child dealing with cerebral palsy and autism, along with our five new young guests. Moreover, my wonderful husband and I owned and operated a custom cabinet/woodworking business that also required a lot of attention.

> *It was 2006 when we received a knock at our door.*

We were able to stay strong mentally through prayer, meditation, reading the Word of God, and ministering to our guest family. It helps when you take your eyes off of "self" and assist others in their time of need. The mother and I grew closer as friends as the months went by. This was a godsend, as it prepared us to be there for one another when times grew even more difficult and challenging. We had no idea what surprise was lurking around the corner.

In 2007, we had a year we will never forget! Our oldest daughter, who was in middle school, grew very ill, battling high fevers and excessive weight loss. After several doctors' appointments and many tests were performed, we were finally referred to a doctor who was able to get her on the road to discovery. Very weak, our daughter had to undergo a neck biopsy after a lump was discovered. A week passed and we were on pins and needles to hear the results. Well, that dreaded call came and left us speechless. The details will be told in my daughter's forthcoming book. However, I can say that her diagnosis required a year and a half of treatment. She experienced a rough road from middle school on into her first year of high school. Again, we relied on God's love and embraced a *"We never ever quit"* attitude!

> *Months passed and our guests were still living in our home.*

No one can make this up! The year of 2008 came and brought with it even more challenges. However, when your faith is strong and you hold on to God, you will make it through. With that said, the first challenge showed up, and you better believe I held tight to His hand as I met a painful fate! My knee gave way when I stepped off of our dining room step into the family room. I fell and landed on both ankles. My loving husband rushed to the scene and immediately picked me up, sat me down, and packed my ankles and feet with ice.

After sitting in the ER for hours and remaining on ice, I was finally seen by the doctor, who took x-rays, and I was scheduled for surgery. After being bedridden for months, and while being cared for by my husband, "Superman," and trying my best to stay on top of all of the kids' school assignments, I finally was able to get out of bed and continue my work and household duties.

Whew, as I look back on those two years, I wonder how anyone could not believe in God and His Son, Jesus Christ. In Deuteronomy 31, it says, "The Lord Himself goes before you and will be with you; He will never leave you nor forsake you. Do not be afraid; do not be discouraged." And lastly, just know that God has a plan for your life. "'For I know the plans I have for you,' declares the Lord, 'plans to prosper you and not to harm you, plans to give you hope and a future'" (Jeremiah 29:11).

When I ministered to our house guests, I would always tell them, "Never ever give up!" The bible says, in 1 Peter 5:8, "Be sober, be vigilant; because your adversary, the devil, as a roaring lion, walketh about, seeking whom he may devour." Therefore, just know that as you walk with the Lord, you *will* be Victorious!

As 2008 ended and 2009 began, I noticed that amongst all of the busyness in our household, our two families began to bond. We were all able to breathe a sigh of relief and enjoy life a little. This was a good thing, because little did we know that a life-threatening occurrence was about to happen that would require every family member to be accountable for the successful running of our household.

Our two families began to bond.

We had to call upon the Lord for strength, courage, and endurance. Remember, my awesome husband had been the main pillar that held everything together the previous years, of course with God's Hand upon him. In mid-2010, we had to rely upon him and his quiet strength once again as we received the devastating news of a big hard lump on my right breast. I was instructed to immediately go to my doctor's office. I underwent a painful biopsy. The results were devastating. "I'm sorry to tell you, Mr. and Mrs. Dixon, Marcia has a diagnosis of HER2 pos breast cancer that is aggressive and needs to be addressed with urgency."

After hearing this type of news, I was told that it's okay to cry or be upset. But I decided to move forward in positivity and ask for the best treatment options. My treatment plan consisted of two laparoscopies, a mastectomy, and chemotherapy, followed by breast reconstruction. My strong mindset and positive attitude came from being close to God and becoming a disciple of Christ, not just a Christian in name only.

Once upon a time, before I came to know the Lord intimately, I was fearful of ever getting cancer. I used to say, *"How can anyone deal with having cancer. Wow, I never want that to happen to me!"* Well it did, but praise God, I felt the loving embrace of the Lord surrounding me every step of the way, therefore *I did not fear!*

Another blessing I experienced was God's guidance on how to creatively wrap my bald head. A few months after I started chemotherapy treatments, I began losing my long hair. At first I felt sad but before I allowed myself to get lost in negative thoughts, I prayed and shifted my focus. "Praise God, I'm alive and I look pretty fashionable with my new head wraps." Strangers who didn't know I had cancer actually thought I was simply wearing a new style. Eventually, I became comfortable being bald and wearing beautiful head scarfs. Remember, it is important to intentionally focus on the positive. This takes a decision to work on strengthening your mindset.

Although I endured a year of chemotherapy and Herceptin IV treatment, through the strength and power of God, I was able to encourage and minister to other patients in the treatment center on infusion days. When friends would ask Pastor P, my pastor at that time, "How's Marcia? It's so sad that she's going through this," she used to tell them to call me, but expect to hear a sermon. I was determined to be healed and whole.

I knew deep inside that God would see me through. I experienced many days of feeling very sick and I didn't think I could go on, but I did! To God be the glory! My response to others who approached me with a sad look was to say, *"I'm fine. I ain't goin' nowhere!"*

I have a wonderful husband, five beautiful children, and a ministry to launch. "I AIN'T GOIN' NOWHERE!"

They would just look at me in amazement. *Making the decision to be filled with the spirit of God and resting in His embrace will carry you through any devastating situation. Just be intentional about allowing God to lead you and guide you and carry you through to victory!*

I must also mention the loving words my wonderful husband said to me after my breast reconstruction surgery. When I was concerned about my appearance because my breast looked uneven and scarred, he replied, "Marcia, I am not concerned about your outward appearance, I am just thankful you are alive!" Wow, that pushed me right back to where I needed to be—focused on being thankful, positive, and moving ahead.

Now, I have a question for you. Are you eating life, or death?

Just as your tongue can speak life or death into a situation, your mouth can physically eat foods that cause the body harm. Through the years, God has revealed to me that foods that are wholesome— one-ingredient foods such as fresh fruits, fresh vegetables, free-range chicken and turkey, wild-caught fish, seeds, lentils, and beans—will nourish your body. Whereas packaged foods, fast foods, sugars, white flour, and dairy products are toxic. Years of eating in an unhealthy manner can lead to major diseases. So begins the journey of what led me to a devastating cancer diagnosis.

Are you eating life? Or death?

More than 30 years ago, I attended a holistic seminar and an appointment with a naturopathic doctor. With careful examination and tests, and after reviewing a questionnaire about my daily activities, it was determined that my lifestyle, stress, and eating habits had to improve. Back then, the doctor even said if my lifestyle did not improve, I could be faced with major health challenges, even the possibility of the dreaded word "cancer."

Well, for a while I took supplements and ate a little better, but not on a consistent basis. I continued to hear and read the latest news on living healthy, exercising regularly, getting good sleep, avoiding stress, and so on. Despite having a desire to do better, I allowed the distractions of life and busyness to cause me to live on "auto-pilot" without stopping to truly examine my life choices. Therefore, I did not make that change.

I came close once, praying, "I know I need to stop eating like this and improve my lifestyle." But I was all talk and no action.

I had much knowledge and understanding. I surrounded myself with positive contacts and attended several lifestyle improvement seminars. I even changed my menu for a while. So, what was missing? It was five things:

- Strong determination
- Being intentional
- Creating a plan
- Staying focused
- *Taking action*

I forgot to turn off the "auto-pilot" and go on "manual." I needed to manually take control of my life, be intentional about it, and do the right things for the right reasons, and expect the right results!

Focus on the results you desire. Remember, it takes more than just *wanting* to do better. When your "auto-pilot" is in control, you tend to go through life without stopping to reflect or make necessary changes. You say, "I know... I'll do it tomorrow." The problem is, tomorrow rarely comes. Days come and go and you are still in the mindset of "getting around to doing better." In order to make lasting change and truly improve your lifestyle, you must *take action!* As a famous pastor and author once said, "Talk about it, think about it. Think about it, talk about it. When does it ever change? Where's the action?"

God wants the best for all of His children. Unfortunately, as we keep going down the wrong road, He has no choice but to allow us to sometimes experience hardship in order to get our attention, as in my case. After years of stress, poor eating and sleeping habits, and little to no exercise, I developed a life-threatening illness, cancer. I am so thankful that by God's grace, mercy, and love, I was healed and made whole. I became consciously conscious instead of walking through life unconsciously unconscious and on auto-pilot.

I woke up! I became intentional and determined to improve my lifestyle, eating, and exercise habits, ready to implement my many years of research and the study of the human mind, speech, and focus. Through this painful journey, I was resurrected and grew stronger and wiser every day. I give all of the credit to my Lord and Savior, Jesus Christ!

I have learned to listen, study, and obey. I accept that I went through this journey, survived, and am now healthy, restored, and whole as an *overcomer*, all so I can share the good news: God has immense love for *you*. Moreover, there is a customized lifestyle plan for you to follow that leads to total health and wholeness! You can learn how to detox and rebuild so you can "Rise And Be Healed"... *spirit, mind, and body!* God gave me this as a theme for my ministry. I love seeing people overcome and grow and glow for Jesus!

I was inspired by another God-given success nugget for life: Decide, then do. It's all up to you. Mindset is *key* if you want to live and walk *free*.

Mindset has the single most powerful influence on a person's success, whether personal or professional. Be determined to develop a positive growth mindset. Where your focus goes, your energy flows. So, decide to be intentional about focusing on becoming totally cleansed and whole in your spirit, mind, and body.

This is what I did to rise and be healed of cancer. Every now and then, I relapse and go back to unhealthy habits. I learned not to condemn myself, but to go to God in prayer and forgive myself so I can begin again. When you condemn yourself and tear yourself down for missing the mark, it not only leaves a scar but opens up a door for the enemy of your soul—the devil—to enter in and harass and oppress you. Do not allow this cycle to start!

As soon as you feel weak, or you miss the mark, go to the Lord in prayer. Begin again!

What I recently added to this mix is to get an accountability partner. This can be a close friend you ask for guidance and encouragement, or a total health coach such as myself. My God-given purpose and mission is to help as many individuals as possible who are ready to go from *OK to Excellent in Spirit, Mind, and Body.* My family and I went through all of these painful life events for a reason—to learn and grow and to be made strong in order to help others to rise up and become *Overcomers!* When I encounter people who are down, depressed, and experiencing devastation, it brings me great joy when they decide to grab ahold of God, develop a positive attitude, and focus on overcoming.

Are you ready to go from "OK" to "Excellent"?

Remember, "With men this is impossible, but with God all things are possible!" (Matthew 19:26).

"For whatever is born of God overcomes the world; and this is the victory that has overcome the world—our faith" (1 John 5:4).

In closing, I will present some more divinely inspired "Nuggets for life" that came from on high. These are intended to encourage, edify, and transform your life. They truly caused me to triumph over setbacks, adversities, devastation, and yes, even cancer! Before you read them, get comfortable in a quiet place, sit still, and meditate on these morsels.

※

In order to walk as an *Overcomer*, you must first be *intentional*, intent on winning. *Decide* to press on and gain control of the challenge you are being faced with, no matter the pain, the cost, or the length of time. Your action must be to press toward the Victor's Crown. I've heard it said by well-known motivational speaker, Les Brown, long ago that, "You don't get what you want in life. You get who you are!" So *decide* to be and walk as an *Overcomer*. Overcomers do not just survive, they thrive! Lastly, and very key, survivors are victimized, but Overcomers are victorious! Survivors have wounds, while Overcomers have scars, just like our Lord and Savior, Jesus Christ.

※

The Word of God tells us in Revelation 12:11 that they overcame by the blood of the Lamb, and the word of their testimony. Therefore, if you are not a believer in Christ Jesus, ask Jesus to be the Lord of your life and repent of your sins. Then thank Him for saving you!

Congratulations, you are now a part of God's kingdom family. *Decide* to fully commit to following Jesus, reading your bible daily, developing a prayer life, having fellowship with other strong believers who bear "good fruit," and spending quality time in God's presence, speaking to Him, worshiping Him, and listening to His voice. Make it your goal to mature as a child of God and study the culture of the kingdom of God. Practice giving your testimony on how God saved you!

Here's something exciting to look forward to as a child of God. Listen to what God promised in Revelation 3:21:

The Lord promised us, "To him that overcometh will I grant to sit with Me in My throne, even as I also overcame, and am set down with My Father in His throne." Wow! As an *Overcomer*, I look forward to the opportunity of being in His Presence around His Throne. What an awesome privilege we have as an *overcoming* believer.

※

*Next, the proper *mindset* is key to walk and live free. Making the time to invest in self-development is paramount! In all my years of studying different types of mindsets, I found that having a growth mindset can lead you to successfully overcoming life's challenges. I adopted this mindset when I was diagnosed with cancer. I *decided* to develop this growth mindset. I also decided to stay focused on the positive. I learned through observing others who were dealing with illness and challenges, that the people who complained and were doubtful were less likely to overcome their challenge and experience any joy in their life. The choice is yours!

Lastly, remember that words are powerful. God spoke the world into existence using words. Words can edify and encourage, but they can also destroy and tear down.

Here's a word of caution: Don't get hung by your tongue! With our tongue we can speak words of life and love, or we can choose to speak words of death and defeat. God once told me, "Speak what you want to happen!" Moreover, the word of God speaks about not focusing on your negative circumstance. Where your focus goes, your energy flows! Focus on using your tongue like a paintbrush and paint the chapters of your life as you desire them to be.

My mission is to encourage, empower, educate, and guide those individuals who are ready to go from "OK to Excellent in Spirit, Mind, and Body." Allow me to partner with you on your journey to total health and wholeness. John 5:6 says, "Do you want to be made whole?"

Decide then do.
It's all up to you.
Mindset and taking action is key
If you want to live and walk free!

~Shalom

Marcia Dixon

Daughter of the Most High God,
Disciple of Jesus and Kingdom Builder

"Blessed be the Lord, Because He has heard the voice of my supplications! The Lord is my strength and my shield; My heart trusted in Him, and I am helped; Therefore my heart greatly rejoices, and with my song I will praise Him."
—Psalm 28:6-7

As a cancer overcomer, total health coach, spiritual ambassador, and entrepreneur, MARCIA D. DIXON is always ready to empower, edify, educate, encourage, and guide individuals into Total Wholeness. "Do you want to be made whole?" —John 5:6

Marcia has been happily married to her husband for 34 years and has five phenomenal children. Her third child is dealing with several special needs and requires around the clock supervision. Despite the demands of raising a disabled child, she and her husband give all five children lots of love, direction, spiritual guidance, and all they need to flourish!

Marcia holds a Bachelor of Science degree in Marketing and Management, and a Bachelor of Arts degree in Theology. She is the Founder and Spiritual Ambassador of Rise And Be Healed

Ministries. She also assists her brother, Senior Pastor of The Victory Zone Christian Fellowship International, as Associate Pastor.

Currently Marcia works as President of Sales and Affiliate Programs for Ijascode Handsoff Marketing System. She's also the founder and Total Health Coach of One Life International, an extension of Rise And Be Healed Ministries, with the mission of coaching and consulting individuals ready to go from OK to Excellent in spirit, mind, and body. She believes God wants us all to live abundantly and to detox and rebuild, so we can rise and be healed—spirit, mind, and body!

If you are ready to grow to the next level spiritually, mentally, and physically, contact Marcia at:

riseandbehealed777@gmail.com

(805) 824-1252

The End... But at What Cost?

Patience Behymer

MY MOTHER AND I BEGAN TO VISIT A COUNSELOR when I was 11 years old after she discovered that I was being sexually abused by my stepfather. It wasn't long before our counselor enlisted the help of a psychiatrist who had mentored him. After a few years of individual sessions, the psychiatrist felt it would be beneficial for us to have joint visits. This simply meant that my mom and I would have one session every couple of weeks together. This created an open forum where we were able to discuss many things that we wouldn't have otherwise.

It was there I began to learn that my mother had been raised in a home where she suffered a great deal of abuse from several family members, and that countless generations of our family before us had shared similar stories and histories. Along the way, my mother revealed to me that her first memories were of severe physical pain inflicted by my grandmother at a young age and that she wasn't even able to remember a time prior to my grandfather's sexual abuse.

All that my mother endured led her to multiple attempts to end her own life. She merely endeavored to escape the relentless agony that consumed her. Sadly, suicide seemed the most logical choice. If she were dead then no one could cause her any further harm.

Even to this day, knowing how these thoughts consumed her fills me with an inexplicable pain. I loved her, and still do, so dearly and deeply. It is a love that my mother was never capable of fully receiving from me. Because of the abuse she suffered throughout her life, especially as a child, she wasn't able to comprehend the unconditional love of her own daughter. The concept of being worthy was so foreign to her that I am unsure if she ever honestly grasped that people could have true affection for her.

My mother began contemplating death when she was a small child. This continued through her adult years and into the final months of her life. I have been told the story of her first suicide attempt more than once, both by my mother and my grandmother on separate occasions and the details overlap. It breaks my heart each time I recollect the tale. In fact, I have grown accustomed to the ache.

> *Countless generations of our family shared similar stories.*

My mom first decided that it would be better for her to die than to live while she was just five years old. She thought about it for some time and selected a course of action—she chose starvation. One day, she just stopped eating. She refused all food.

After the first three days of her hunger strike, my grandmother began to be concerned. By the fourth day, my mother had very little energy and remained in her bedroom. After some contemplation, my grandmother chose to cook my mom's favorite food in the hopes it would entice her to eat something.

The next morning my grandma cooked an entire package of bacon, just a couple of pieces at a time, because she knew that the aroma would fill the entire apartment. She thought the smell would attract my mother's attention and draw her into the kitchen.

Still, my mother did not come out of her room. So my grandmother laid all of the bacon on a plate that she set on a small table in the hall across from my mom's bedroom. There the bacon sat for many hours until my mother could not handle the smell any longer.

I remember her explaining that smelling the bacon cooking had made her so hungry that her stomach began to hurt. She continued to lay in her bed until she was completely overwhelmed. Her stomach had been growling for hours and she crept out of her room. When she saw that no one was around, she devoured every bit of the bacon. She even licked the grease off of her fingers. Then she simply returned to her bed.

♦ Patience Behymer

When my grandmother discovered the empty plate later, she was relieved. She had been worried that my mom would only eat a slice or two to curb the intense hunger she knew she must have been feeling. When the plate was empty, my grandmother knew the worst of the struggle was over because all of the bacon was gone.

My grandma confessed years later that she did not understand that my mom was trying to die at that time. My mother was always capable of great stubbornness. Because of this, my grandmother assumed she had gotten upset or angry about something and was protesting whatever it had been by not eating.

The two never discussed the incident until my mom was an adult since she had resumed eating meals as usual, and my grandma didn't want to make a big deal or encourage her to behave that way in the future.

I don't have any memories of my mother injuring herself during my childhood, and I can't retell any other suicide attempts she made during her own childhood or teen years because none were ever shared with me, but I do know that she made more than one attempt prior to her pregnancy with me when she was 20.

That being said, the reality was that there was a possibility that she may harm herself and it hung in the air continually. I always understood we needed to care for my mother and be careful because she may make sudden and rash decisions. It's difficult to explain how I knew this because no one in my family ever said this to me. It was simply the general environment in which I grew up. It was like a shadow that we all lived under.

It was like a shadow we all lived under.

There was a short reprieve from the intense stress and fear this consistently caused me. I had the privilege of experiencing a few years of relief. There was a time period in which my mother was not allowed to harm herself. It actually became a term of her continued treatment.

The restriction was made by our psychiatrist. In order to remain in therapy, my mother would not be permitted to make any destructive and volatile choices. She was required to sign a contract, and one of the agreements was that she needed to reach out before she did anything drastic or made any rash decisions. I still remember how hard it was for her to make the commitment to us.

The doctor presented her with some paperwork during one of our joint sessions one day. He asked her to read it and she grew very quiet. He explained to her it was for her protection, and mine as well. She became emotional. I remember he needed to make it completely clear that he would not continue to see her if she was unwilling to agree to the new terms.

She was in tears and I held my breath. I watched as she finally signed the forms and handed them back to the doctor. I took a deep breath and could not stop smiling. I think she may have thought I was laughing at her or mocking her in some fashion. This was not true. I think it was the closest to happiness I had ever felt.

> *She was in tears and I held my breath.*

It was because of this that I was able to recognize the cloud that had been hanging over me like an eternally ominous threat throughout my young life. Prior to this it was so normal that I never even realized it had been there. I was so pleased. I literally felt safer and lighter while my mother silently drove away from the office that day.

Our doctor had responded to something my mom had shared during one of their individual visits. They had discussed a recent attempt that she hadn't shared with anyone. She had not required any medical treatment and neither of them ever discussed any of the details with me. I never was made aware if she required any immediate assistance from him but what I do know is that I did not have to think about the possibility of her harming herself for some time.

That reprieve ended when I was 16 years old. Our psychiatrist was offered a position in another state which he accepted. It was extremely emotional for my mother and me. We both relied so heavily on him and his care for us. This was especially true for my mom. His treatment truly transformed our lives. I would not be the person I am now without the years I was able to spend in therapy with him.

With the contract no longer in place, my mother had no recourse or active plan of action for when she was struggling. This was an intensely deep blow for me. I became aware of an exceptionally stark reality—how little importance my presence made in my mom's life. After our doctor moved, she felt and said how very little she had to live for. Her words cut me so deeply. I often still feel the pain when I pause to think of it. For many years I felt it physically.

Our psychiatrist had been a vital stability for my mother, and the emotional anguish of him leaving made the simplest parts of her life seem insurmountable. Her first re-attempt was after I turned 17. She chose to overdose by taking the entire bottle of one of her medications. Her husband at that time did not handle the situation well and I was left with the responsibility of saving her life and getting her the medical treatment she needed.

I came into the living room late one evening and asked my stepfather where my mother was. He was eating a snack and watching television. He informed me that she was probably in bed because she had taken pills. I asked if she was okay and he responded that he didn't know. He never looked at me.

I was fuming and my heart raced as I quietly prepared for the worst. I headed to their bedroom to check on her. She was despondent and admitted to taking the medicine. I was relieved to be aware of the situation in time. I left her in bed, walked back to the living room, and asked my stepfather what he was going to do. He said he wasn't going to do anything. He said something about her wanting to die. He seemed angry with her. I did not sense any compassion or concern whatsoever.

I quietly prepared for the worst.

I already didn't have much respect for my stepdad because I had witnessed him treat people quite horribly when we were in stores and restaurants. This was the last straw. I felt something rise up from within me I had never felt before. I believe it was strength followed by courage. I wasn't able to drive yet but I told him that if he did not get up right now and take my mother to the hospital then I would drive her there myself. I knew he was concerned about what I would tell them once we got there.

He got up and took us. I half expected him to drop us off and then go home but he didn't. I have very little memory of the rest of that night or the following few days. We did get my mother to the hospital in time and she survived without any permanent injury.

Something broke inside me that night which remains to this day. Her overwhelming desire to die spoke volumes to me concerning my value and left me questioning my self-worth. It was such a painful reality for me. This hurt deeply and left me feeling abandoned. If my mother was willing to leave me, then I knew that no one would ever stay. If she couldn't love me, then how could anyone?

My mother always told me how much she loved me, what a blessing I was to her, and how I was her angel... but her actions painted an entirely different picture. Despite her words, it was evident that I was actually inconsequential. The way I internalized my mother's personal struggles was to view my existence as meaningless. She knew I had no one else in the world besides her. I believed that I was not worth fighting for or alongside.

> *Something broke inside me that night.*

When I was young, I was unable to remove myself from the equation. If she had ever been successful, I would be entirely orphaned. I was so greatly hurt and confused because this didn't appear to be a factor in her decision-making process. I thought that she must not love me if she was willing to leave me.

My mother was a tortured and broken woman who had suffered greatly throughout her life. Her various attempts were merely a way for her to escape the pain and anguish she constantly lived with. She was also addicted to various substances. She was under the influence of something the majority of my life. Suicide and addiction made her seem selfish from my perspective. The reality that my mother chose death over life has had a profound impact on me, causing severe emotional wounds.

I don't think she ever fully understood the impact all of this had on me. She seemed to be able to separate herself from me emotionally and viewed much of her responsibility toward me like a job without being able to recognize my need to have a solid relationship with her—an authentically deep connection which I desperately needed. I longed to feel my mother's love and to know that she was proud of me. I wished so badly to know what she thought of me. She simply was closed off the majority of the time.

My mother's mental health continued to decline. She divorced my stepfather and remarried an even more abusive man. Finally, they moved across the country after a few tumultuous years. Doctors there cared for her and highly medicated her, which made it even more difficult for her to function. She received very little therapy.

I was notified every time she had a reattempt. Somewhere along the way I actually lost count. I had to ask her husband and other family members to please stop notifying me unless it was tragic. I simply could not emotionally handle the stress of it all. And there was nothing I could do because I lived too far away.

Eventually my mother grew very ill. She developed emphysema after smoking for the majority of her life. I had to move her across the country again in order for me to care for her. Of course we didn't know it was to be her final year.

Doctors ordered her to stop smoking entirely but she did not see the point of that. She needed to use oxygen continuously because her lung function was so low. She could barely walk around the house and was unable to do any cooking or cleaning for herself.

One day I took her shopping. She had been living with me for about a month and she requested to buy cigarettes along with the other things she needed. I explained to her that this wasn't allowed. This made her very angry. She barricaded herself in her bedroom after we got home.

My family and I had to go out for several hours. While I was concerned about her, there was little I could do because she refused to open her door or speak with me. It was Halloween night and my son had a football game in another city. My kids wanted to spend the night at their aunt's house, which was a blessing because I had no idea how my mother would behave when I returned home. She could be pretty volatile, even violent.

When my husband and I arrived, we found her unresponsive. The table remained in front of her bedroom door so my husband pushed it out of the way. We discovered that she had consumed all of the medication she was currently prescribed. I had just recently refilled them because it was nearing the first of the month. At that time she was taking anywhere from 10 to 12 different medications.

She was lying in bed and I found a note she had written to us explaining that she wanted to die. We knew it would be faster to drive her to the hospital than to wait for an ambulance. I began to get her up out of bed and she told me to leave her to die. At some point I completely lost it. I became so angry that I couldn't see. Everything went black. I got really rough with her, pulling her up out of the bed. My husband stopped me because she was so frail and thin. He was concerned I would hurt her. He spoke to me and I returned to the moment. He said he would walk her out to the car.

I remember taking a breath and asking the Lord to help me. I couldn't even move from where I was standing. I felt a peace flow through me and I took another deep breath. And then a couple more. I was able to walk into the hall and met them at our front door. My husband looked over my mother and asked, "Are you with me?" and I was able to answer yes and nod my head. Then I saw him relax. We got her into the car and as we drove the ten minutes to the hospital she kept telling us to just leave her and that she just wanted to die. It was the longest ten minutes of my life.

> *I remember taking a breath and asking the Lord to help me.*

At the hospital the situation grew more dire. It was too late for them to give her anything to make her vomit up the medications. Only time would tell. She wound up living through the night but needed dialysis each day for three days. She survived, but just barely.

Because of the emphysema, my mother required many other hospitalizations. Her final suicide attempt actually occurred in the hospital. I was not present but arrived shortly afterward and was given the details firsthand by her nurse who was visibly shaken.

He recounted that my mother had just finished eating lunch. She asked for an ice cream. She was happy when he brought it to her. He returned to check on her a few minutes later and found her with a plastic bag wrapped around her head. He was able to remove it. She was not injured and did not require any resuscitation because it had been such a short time. The staff could not figure out where she had gotten the bag from. They finally asked her. It was the bag from her trash can which had not been anywhere near her bed. She was not able to get in and out of bed or walk to the restroom without assistance. She had managed somehow to retrieve the bag from the trash can. To this day we don't know how. She never did explain.

The following year she passed away from complications from the emphysema. As I grew older, I began to understand that during a crisis my mother was not thinking about me or any other repercussion for her choices. She simply wished for the emotional torture and pain within her to stop. That being said, with each new attempt I felt the wounds as though I had been slashed deeply. After many years I no longer knew how to protect myself and care for my mother. I understand now that one person cannot be responsible for another—especially if they are not contributing to their self-care. As a young adult, I had to begin distancing myself from her. This caused another layer of pain. It was a dual-edged sword. On one hand I felt like a failure, and on the other I was convinced that my mother would rather remain in her mess than learn how to be healthier so we could mend our broken lives together.

Over the last decade I have been able to heal, and while it is still very sad to me, I understand that the burden is not mine to bear. While there are scars that remain, I no longer feel the sting of pain when a memory arises. The Lord has used the love of friendship to help resolve that my beliefs about my lack of worth were highly unfounded. My mother's inability to cherish me well was based in her inability to accept herself and was never an accurate measure of my lovability at all. While I did not receive the deep love I so desperately needed from my mom, Jesus has loved me so thoroughly that I am able to love others wholeheartedly.

Patience Behymer

PATIENCE BEHYMER is a victorious overcomer who has experienced deep and lasting freedom through the gospel of Jesus Christ. She has tenderly cultivated an intimate relationship with the Holy Spirit. She is a generous encourager who enjoys mentoring others and has a passion for showing the healing and restorative love of Jesus.

Facebook.com/profile.php?id=100090017498596

Instagram.com/patiencesrose/

"Show Me, Right Now!"

Amy Charbonneau

I SAT ON THE FLOOR OF MY KITCHEN, consumed by despair and hopelessness. "How did I end up here? My son deserves a better mother. The world would be better off without me."

These thoughts, along with countless others, bombarded my mind like an all-out assault. I couldn't pinpoint the exact time, but it must have been around 1:00 in the morning. The darkness outside matched the heaviness in my heart, and an eerie silence filled the air.

I barely knew my neighbors, except for the nosy lady at the end of the block who kept an eye on the homeowner's association. Everyone seemed to keep to themselves, me included, never making an effort to connect with one another.

Anger coursed through my veins, leaving me disillusioned and devoid of purpose.

There I sat, clutching a knife and a bottle of pain pills. It was a desperate impulse, a poorly conceived plan to swallow the pills and then cut my wrist. I hadn't thought it through; it was just an act of desperation.

Silent tears streamed down my face as I cried, my head resting against the stove. With the pills in my hand, I closed my eyes and uttered a prayer, though it bore little resemblance to any prayer I had ever heard.

"Well, if you truly love me, then show me," I pleaded, the underlying message being, *"Show me right now!"*

"Show Me, Right Now!" ◆

I'm aware that people often advise against making demands on God. After all, He is God. But in moments of desperation, rational thoughts fade away. You simply speak or act, without considering the consequences of your words or actions.

Almost immediately after uttering those words, my toddler son emerged from his bedroom, sleepy-eyed but determined. He spotted me and crawled into my lap.

"I love you, Mommy!" he exclaimed.

A floodgate of emotions burst open within me, and I wept uncontrollable tears—years of pent-up emotions came pouring out. My sweet little boy became the instrument of God's affection, forever altering the course of my life.

The next day, as I dropped my son off with my mother, who was his babysitter at the time, Jesus showed up again—this time through my mom. She shared a Bible study happening at her church and offered to watch my son so I could attend without feeling pressured by her presence. Looking back, it was a selfless act of love from a mother who recognized my need for something I wouldn't receive from her at that moment.

> *Years of pent-up emotions came pouring out.*

Uncertain and overwhelmed by insecurities, fear, and doubt, I attended the study. Coincidentally, it focused on the book of Job (in the Old Testament of the Bible), which may not be familiar to everyone. In the opening chapter, there's a scene where Satan stands before God, and they engage in a dialogue. It seems as if God throws Job under the bus by presenting Satan with an opportunity to do what he liked to Job, except take his life.

In that moment, rage consumed me. How could God allow such horrors to befall Job? How could a *loving* God let that happen?

At the time, I possessed an unhealthy understanding of who God is. I cried, questioned, yelled, and stormed out of the room multiple times, but the woman leading the study embodied Jesus' love.

She gave me the space I needed to express my anger, confusion, and hurt. As I grappled with those emotions, she remained calm, speaking softly, and assuring me of God's immeasurable love.

For reasons beyond my comprehension, I continued attending the study, completing *most of* the workbook assignments and engaging in conversations with God.

The art of prayer is unique to everyone, but there is a common thread—we often talk *at* God, or we become willing participants, both speaking and listening to His voice.

I confess it took time for me to learn to listen. It required developing an understanding of who God is and who we are as His children. Trauma often instills a sense of worthlessness, creating a chasm we must bridge. The truth is, Jesus has already built the bridge; we are often just blind to it.

> *It took time for me to learn to listen.*

The bridge that takes us from darkness to light is ultimately our encounters with the people of God. Sometimes, you encounter individuals who help you take each brave step forward. Other times, you encounter people who are quick to remind you of your failures. I have been both that person and the recipient of that pain.

In January 2023, I was preparing to speak in the Philippines, to a small church in the heart of a big city. As I talked with God about what He wanted me to share, I had a vision (like a dream, but awake), and I saw this vast black void. It felt cold, and lifeless. Then I looked to the right and saw this vast expanse of light, full of vibrance and the feeling that "I want to be there."

Between the dark void and the light place, there was a chasm.

Across that chasm was a bridge made of *living stones* (1 Peter 2). What was interesting was how some were held with mortar and others were just sitting there, not connected.

Suddenly, a brave person wanted to go from the darkness to the light, and they began to step onto the bridge. As they stepped, some stones moved in a way that propelled them forward, yet others would crumble beneath their feet and cause them to stumble.

I began to talk with God about this imagery. He showed me that the mortar was His grace and love, strong enough to hold stones together and bear up under the weight of another's burdens.

The stones that crumbled were not mortared into the whole. As they crumbled under that weight, the person stumbled, sometimes falling so often they ended up turning back to the darkness.

Who we encounter on the journey matters. Sometimes we meet those who propel us forward, and other times it's someone who causes us to turn back in disbelief and hopeless despair.

In that moment, I knew my calling was to help others get from the darkness to the light and to help them be mortared into the bridge by the grace, love, and mercy of Jesus.

Inner Healing: The Treacherous Path Forward

The journey of renewing your mind may span a lifetime, but certain aspects of your past can be transformed today. You can reshape and dismantle the blockages in your thinking, redirecting yourself away from destructive thought patterns.

Neuroplasticity is an incredible science, and the abundant research available on the internet can offer helpful and encouraging insights.

There are traumas that are so deep we need the help of someone outside of ourselves and our circle to help us navigate the path out. For me, that was a Christian counselor who specialized in EMDR (Eye Movement Desensitization and Reprocessing) therapy. Up to that point I had attended conferences meant to help me heal (and truth be told, they peeled back layers), but I had not been able to make my heart and brain connect in an emotionally healthy way with those really painful past memories. My past involved sexual abuse, a belief that I was unworthy of love, as well as divorce, abortion, remarriage, adoption, and a blended family, all trying to figure out how to be "the good Christian girl" and model something that looked like love.

My first encounter with renewing my mind was at a deliverance weekend. My husband and I went through five bible study sessions about why people need deliverance, and then traveled to a place in another state for an intensive retreat. Although I experienced much healing during that event, the way I viewed myself and my relationship with Jesus was not changed. Even as burdens began to lift and I delved into the Scriptures, something still hindered my ability to release deep pain and love others the way Jesus loved me.

1 Corinthians 13:4-7 beautifully describes love, and we can read it with God in the place of love. God is patient, God is kind... This is a beautiful devotional time and helpful for learning about God's nature. I encourage you to open a bible, or the Bible app and try it!

Something still hindered my ability to release deep pain.

According to 1 John 4:17b, there is this invitation that can be completely misunderstood: we are like God—*As He is, so are we!* If I take that idea, I return to 1 Corinthians 13 and read it with my own name in the place of love. *Amy is patient, Amy is kind... Amy does not keep a record of wrongs...*

Wait...what????? Gulp—I'm supposed to be patient, kind, and um... not keep a record of wrongs (among other things)???

"But God, what about (so-and-so)? Have you forgotten what they did to me? How can I forget that?" Painful memories of past encounters flooded my mind at an overwhelming pace.

Yet our loving Father, full of patience, sends His Spirit to guide us into all truth (John 16). I experienced a series of events in my life that forced me to confront unhealed trauma within myself and the reality that I harbored feelings of hatred toward another human being—something completely out of character for me, terrified me. I genuinely love people! All people. Hearing their stories fascinates me and fills me with inspiration. But a relationship in my life pushed me into the depths of old pain.

It's astonishing what a single moment can do.

Sitting in a circle surrounded by people striving to love better, I confessed, "I hate him."

Love stands as the antithesis of hate. God is love. To hate another is to oppose God's heart for them. As I poured out my frustrations about this person to God, I reached a point of complete surrender.

"I can't do it," I admitted.

In a gentle and tender whisper, the Spirit responded, *"You're right, but I can."* He gently guided me toward three pivotal catalysts that would set me on a path of profound inner healing: a transformative conference in Portland, Oregon; the enlightening Power Encounters course during my master's studies; and the invaluable support of a Christian counselor skilled in EMDR therapy. Let me take a moment to delve into each of these catalysts, unveiling their significance in my healing journey.

> *"I can't do it,"*
> *I admitted.*

The conference in Portland, aptly named Compassion to Action, proved to be a turning point. This gathering, led by a passionate Christian group, focused on identity in Christ, immersing oneself in the Spirit's fiery power, and sharing the testimony of Jesus with others. Though I was familiar with the teachings, it was here that I encountered the presence of God in a profoundly transformative way. Enveloped in His presence, it felt like stepping into a room where the air itself was different—thicker, more alive. As the teachings flowed and prayers were lifted, the world around me faded, leaving me face to face with God. His consuming fire ignited a new sense of purpose, incinerating the barriers that hindered my growth and freedom in Him. I found myself in a fetal position on the floor, seriously ugly-crying!

Dignity? What's that?

During that conference, locked away with God, I could not have cared less about what anyone thought of this 40-something-year-old woman, mom of five, sobbing uncontrollably! Perhaps that is one of the keys to the unlocking I experienced?

No fear of what anyone else thought about my life, my story, my pain or how I handled (or mishandled) any of it. This was major step one!

Step two showed up unexpectedly. A friend shared about a Christian counselor proficient in EMDR therapy. This method resonated with me, and I embarked on a transformative journey with her, attending seven sessions over two months. Through this process, I realized that I was engaged in a dance with Jesus Himself. Painful memories were unveiled, and I met Him within those very moments. As tears flowed, I offered up my pain, visualizing the act of surrendering these burdens to Him, allowing Him to carry them far away.

In tandem, I explored the realms of inner healing prayer during my master's studies, a model that shared similarities with EMDR therapy. This revelation dawned upon me—sitting with Jesus and working through my struggles was a possibility at any given time. The intricate dance between our natural existence and our spiritual essence began to take shape, offering a pathway to wholeness and restoration.

Indeed, the journey toward inner healing unfolded gradually over eight years, culminating in a transformative year where the embrace of Jesus, inner healing prayer, EMDR therapy, and self-discovery brought about immediate shifts within me. Even my husband noticed the change in my responses to various situations. It was a testament to the profound and rapid impact of God's love in our lives. This process doesn't merely change the mind—it transforms the heart, a shift that ripples through our identity, beliefs, and perception of the world.

> *The omnipotent love of God extends to both the wounded and the wounding.*

During this metamorphosis, one truth shone brightly: the omnipotent love of God extends to both the wounded and the wounding. This revelation sparked a personal revolution within me, inspiring forgiveness, and responsibility. Through deep and intentional engagement with Scripture, I uncovered a loving God free from judgment and condemnation. Jesus, the embodiment of divine love, revealed the path to genuine connection. Engaging with Him wasn't merely a spiritual exercise—it had a scientific counterpart known as mutual mind-state, a profound connection formed through intimate relationships.

As I embraced this transformative communion with God, my perspective shifted. He became my confidant, my companion in facing hurt, fears, and joys. His perspective ignited a transformative process, infusing love and grace into painful memories. The outcome was astonishing—painful facts remained, but the emotional chains were broken. Healing, redemption, and renewal blossomed within me, unveiling a new creation, embarking on a brand-new journey.

The process echoed the wisdom of Isaiah 61:3, exchanging mourning for joy, despair for praise. The ashes of my past metamorphosed into a magnificent garden of transformation. The burdens that once defined me melted away as I sought refuge in the arms of Jesus, discovering the power of forgiveness, the gateway to freedom.

Chains relinquished their grip; the prison of the past shattered. Jesus really did come to set the captives free! And He is still freeing his children—you and me.

Romans 12:1-3 reminds us of our purpose—our everyday lives, our very existence, offered as a living sacrifice. Fixing our attention on God, the transformative power of divine love reshapes us from within. Immersed in His grace, we evolve into well-formed maturity.

Embrace the journey of inner healing.

With deep gratitude, I extend a heartfelt invitation. Embrace the journey of inner healing, embrace the transformative power of God's love. Through His presence, through His guidance, and with the testimony of those who have risen from the ashes, you can step out of the shadows of your past into the brilliance of a new beginning.

Amy Charbonneau

AMY CHARBONNEAU is an accomplished professional with a passion for holistic wellness and empowering individuals to rise from the ashes and thrive. With over 23 years of experience in the industry, Amy owns and operates Awaken Joy, LLC: Coaching, Spice Co, and Skincare, where she offers valuable support and guides others on their journey toward wholeness.

Amy's educational background includes a Bachelor's degree in Biblical and Theological Studies from the King's University and a Master's degree in Intercultural Studies from Fuller Theological Seminary. She is currently in a doctoral program with Grand Canyon University. Her love for learning and gaining new perspectives has been a driving force in her personal and professional growth. Amy values the transformative power of education and believes that true change starts with a renewed heart and mind.

When she's not busy with her various ventures, Amy enjoys spending quality time with her loved ones. She finds joy in hiking, watching movies, and going on coffee dates with friends. Adventure and drama are her favorite genres, both in books and movies. Amy's love for exploration has taken her to several countries, including Costa Rica, Mexico, Canada, Germany, France, Greece, Kenya,

Israel, Dominican Republic, Philippines, and Jordan, allowing her to embrace diverse cultures and expand her worldview.

She is a contributing author in these two international bestselling books: *The New Rules of Wellness* and *The Art of Connection*. Through her inspiring work and genuine desire to uplift others, Amy Charbonneau continues to leave a lasting impact on the lives of those she encounters.

mydigitalhomepage.com/amy-charbonneau

MY XCELLENCE MATTERS ON MY PILGRIMAGE TO MEET JESUS

REV. LINDA HOUSDEN

OFTEN AS CHILDREN OF GOD, we allow Satan to bluff and coerce us into submission and defeat when we actually have all the power of the resurrected, victorious Christ living in us, once we seek him in every area of life. It takes complete surrender to know and realize we each have a purpose to fulfill—the Great Commission, as in Matthew 28:18-20, where the risen Lord calls His people to make disciples of all nations as an expression of His supreme authority in heaven and on earth.

A book that impacted my life forever was called *Living for the Promise: The Pursuit of Xcellence*, by Dr. Angella Palmer Banks. It was her personal 10-year journey of self-love, brokenness, depression, and sacrifice to fulfill a dream. I pray that my story of pain while living with a workaholic will be used to glorify God. It is my prayer that you will see that God fulfilled his promises and purpose for my life. It is my source of healing from within that I can even write this message.

At age 71, I am on a pilgrimage to meet Jesus and reminding myself that my Xcellence matters. The markers in our lives remind us we are all travelers. We all have these and it is our journeys that reveal our shortcomings and show us we are not alone in this world.

I was 17 years old when my dear friend Mary prayed with me to invite Jesus into my heart. Soon after I began to assist her in children's church at the Lutheran Church we both attended together. I always believed Jesus loved me, because my sister and I grew up going to church with our neighbor's family. Dad worked

Sundays, but Mom made sure that we both went to church regularly. As a young child I remember well my learning of the song "Jesus Loves Me," and throughout my entire life, the lyrics of this song truly have strengthened me to be the woman of God I am today.

If I take the number 17 and reverse it, it is 71—the age I am now. The one scripture I wish I had understood better much earlier in life is I Peter 1:18. "Your life is a journey, and you must travel with a deep consciousness of God."

To know Him is to spend time with Him, and attending church never provided me with the deep connection with God that I was hungry for. I knew there was more. I came to the realization that I had an incorrect concept of how to use the Bible and for years I used it as if it were an instruction manual, simply picking it up when I felt like it. It was the do's and don'ts book for whenever I needed it, not fully understanding its value—to know God more.

I lost many years lacking the truth of how the Bible is meant to draw us closer to Christ, seeing Him with more clarity and loving Him with more of our affections, with the primary message of the Bible being that the work is already done.

During my first year of college, I became pregnant and was able to hide it for almost five months, not knowing how I would tell my family the news. I experienced shame and pain because my parents indicated they wanted me to give the baby up for adoption. This did not happen because miraculously they had a change of heart once they saw their beautiful grandson, Greg, for the very first time.

> *During my first year of college, I became pregnant.*

I had been admitted for observation prior to giving birth, with toxemia. Little did I know that the night before I was to be released that my parents would call the charge nurse to give me the message they would be coming in late to visit me. This was because they went shopping to purchase an entire nursery set-up for the beautiful five-pound, three-ounce baby boy who would later become the son they never had. I was overwhelmed with gratitude, but it was a traumatic time for me also, with my new life ahead as a young mother.

Overnight, my son had three women rushing to feed him. I had gotten married to my boyfriend Bobby before giving birth, but he eventually moved to Arkansas to be with his family there, so as not to create additional problems. He only had an eighth-grade education, and my parents had educational expectations of their daughters that he respected.

Greg has maintained a relationship with his real dad throughout his life and for this I am grateful. Bobby married again and had two daughters and another son. That son—named Bobby, Jr.—died in a tragic drowning accident at the age of five. After that, I felt I always needed to protect Greg because I knew he was the only biological son Bobby would now ever have.

My son was age 7 when I married my second husband, Ted, who had a 7-year-old daughter and 3-year-old son from a previous marriage of 10 years duration. I imagined how we would become a blended family, respecting each other's values and always building one another up.

When Ted initially asked me out, I replied no. He proceeded to tell me next how he had a glass eyeball, and was going to do whatever he needed to get a yes response. I was a nurse working late shift and would occasionally stop at In-N-Out Burger, where he worked, before going home. I certainly didn't believe Ted had a glass eyeball, but curiosity did kick in. When my car battery died in the drive-through lane, Ted immediately offered to jump start my car. That's how our friendship began.

After meeting over coffee, I learned Ted was the youngest of six children and his biological father was deceased. I also learned his ex-wife had cheated on him, but I believed any man married for ten years had to have some good qualities. Ted was six years older than me. My parents and older sister expressed concern about our "too fast-grown relationship." I questioned my family's assessment.

Ted and I spent our time going to nice restaurants and doing things with the kids when we were off from work. I was especially happy when Ted played basketball with my son, Greg, and paid attention to him. I hoped that if we ever married, he would perhaps consider adopting Greg. I knew Ted had a vasectomy and could no longer have more children, so we also discussed the possibility of having foster children in our home. Ted seemed okay with this, knowing I loved children.

In late 1975, Ted's divorce was finalized and monthly child support payments began for his two children, of which he never missed one payment. Prior to getting married on July 30, 1976, Ted and I saved up enough money for a down payment on our first home in North Hollywood, California. My mom, sister, and I made beautiful peach and white lace decorations. Ted and I decided we wanted our three children to be part of the wedding service. Ted's son, T.J., was shy, so we chose not to force him at just three years of age. Greg was our ring bearer and Cheri was our flower girl. Our two 7-year olds did an amazing job with big smiles on their faces. It was the happiest day I could ever have imagined, even seeing them dance together at the reception.

I believed we would be a Christ-centered family from that day on. It did not happen, though, with many years of enduring physical, emotional, financial, and spiritual hardship, and encounters with God—too many to share in one story.

It was on our honeymoon in Hawaii that I first realized I had married a man with a controlling spirit. I was completely taken offguard when we were looking at the restaurant menu and he said I could have an English muffin. I replied, "What?" Yes, I had heard correctly. This was our first argument and I let him know this was not acceptable. Overall we had a nice time, but with some additional red flag warnings.

Two months after moving to our first home, Ted was transferred to Covina, California, which meant another move. I would be 45 minutes away from my parents' home, and have to commute to my workplace, 45 minutes every day, and utilize a babysitter for my son.

We discussed getting involved in a local church. Ted worked many Sundays, so I began scouting alone for a church we might both like to attend. A neighbor's grandson was Senior Pastor of Faith Community Church in West Covina, which happened to be an offshoot of the Church of Christ. It took some getting used to, but soon we did make FCC our home church for 35 years. Ted was a giver and together we tithed our 10 percent faithfully, and another 10 percent of our monthly earnings to mission outreach. I grew to love the people at FCC and in no time we joined an adult Sunday School class. I served in a variety of areas in the church, and Ted became an usher to help out when he had his off-work days.

There was much to do in our new home to put up brick walls, get window coverings, complete our landscaping, and build a pool. This kept us busy and on our toes. We routinely had Ted's children every weekend or at least every other weekend, as our schedules allowed.

Ted was most definitely a workaholic. He worked six days a week with one day off. I did not feel I could ever nag him about his work habits, because I too sometimes worked double shifts at the hospital like when we met. Work took a toll on our personal lives, but over time I knew he was missing out on having fun together.

I joined a tennis class on Saturdays and got proficient. I wanted for Ted to learn, and so he did. To my surprise, he liked the game and could even beat me. We finally had something we could do together, and at the time it was satisfying.

It was only after a hit-and-run auto accident in 1980 that I cried out to God about my marriage more than ever. My son had a sprained ankle and I sustained a serious head concussion with two fractured ribs. The accident was just the beginning of a series of events that took a huge toll on our marriage. A serious tennis injury put me on crutches and took me out of nursing for two months, only to return to my job and sustain another more complicated work injury. It is believed that I returned too soon after the quad tear injury. I was diagnosed with iliopsoas tendonitis, which I still receive acupuncture and chiropractic care for today. I was sent to doctor after doctor, seeing 54 different medical providers for CT scans, a myelogram, sonograms, ultrasounds, and EMGs. There was no relief from the excruciating pain. I felt as if no one believed me. Pain goes unseen and I did not want to be a burden to Ted. Seeing doctor after doctor made me feel as if I was going crazy, though I did eventually get referred to a most remarkable psychiatrist who became helpful.

There were a total of 7 hospitalizations along my journey of recovery from depression associated with chronic pain syndrome and my rocky road marriage. I went 4 long years being denied permanent disability benefits. I never gave up and sought an attorney who soon advocated on my behalf, due to having chronic pain, fibromyalgia, and associated depression. After the judge released his favorable decision, I inquired why he granted my request when others did not. He shared how his wife had a friend with a similar story but had taken her life. "Linda, you have way too much to give this world that needs you, and I'm going to submit this on your behalf because you have a big assignment ahead of you." I knew he was providing me with a renewed sense of hope for my future.

We stayed active in our church with many challenges in every area of our marriage. Another work transfer took us to Modesto, California, involving the sale of our home and being apart for 7 long months. One of us commuted every weekend that entire time, sometimes with Greg and our two dogs. It was not easy for either of us. I felt this was good for Ted getting a promotion, and I surrendered, knowing a spouse goes where her husband goes. Once our home sold, we moved into a beautiful new 3,000-square-foot home with work to do all over again, and a new community of friends in a new church.

I had a mission trip planned to Russia with our Covina church team, so I went a few months after the move. While in Russia I told my pastor I had an urgency to call home. When I reached Ted I asked one question: "What is going on?" He asked, "How do you know?" I repied, "There is such a thing as the Holy Spirit." He shared how he had been put on suspension from work and an investigation was being conducted. This began another journey of our leaning in to God like never before! When I returned home I learned Ted would be transferred back to southern California because of issues involving a sexual harrassment case brought against him.

The investigation began as a result of a 16-year-old female employee, saying she did not get her movie perk ticket, which in fact she had. On that morning, Ted needed the employees to exit the back room so he could open the safe and begin the daily money count. She was loitering so he put his hand on her shoulder, politely requesting again that she exit. Her father had recently been released from prison, and most likely saw an open door of opportunity to put his daughter through college if she were to sue, which they in fact did do.

Could this really be happening? The In-N-Out owner Rich Snyder had died in a plane crash in 1993, which led to a rapid decline in Ted's confidence and self-esteem. He was given counseling through the company and eventually was terminated. No one manager could compare to Ted's excellent sales volume. He was a champion and others knew it. I will always believe that this incident would not have resulted in my husband's departure from the company (after 32 years of faithful service) had Rich still been alive.

Upon our return to southern California, we were unable to locate another home until we found out the neighbor directly across from our old house was putting theirs on the market. We spent the next 9 years looking at the home I loved across the street.

During this time we became foster parents to 22 special needs infants. I also became a Daycare Director. These were probably the best 9 years in our marriage, because we grew closer to God in our ability to trust Him more in every area of our lives.

We had marital counseling regularly for problems that developed. I eventually moved back home with my mother, and Ted later made the decision to move into a men's shelter. It was a very sad time for us both. I would sometimes drive to his worksites to park, then cry and pray for hours for Ted. I still had love for this man who had been a workaholic in both of his marriages, with two unhappy wives and three children who were now grown adults, having learned difficult lessons and never having experienced the healthy part of having the good father-child relationship they truly deserved. Many times I brought up the topic of adopting Greg, however this never did happen.

To this day I cannot imagine the severe kind of emotional pain Ted must have grown up with. Here I had married a very successful businessman, and yet he lost everything, much like Job in the Bible.

Ted lived with diabetes for many years, and of course I did not win with my nagging him about his smoking habit. One day he fell at the shelter home and gave me the scare of my life with his being unconcious and in ICU for three days. I was summoned immediately and never left his side until God answered my prayer for him to recover fully. This Ted did, and prompted the time we would get back together to live with my mother in her home.

In 2010 I acquired a fixer-upper home as a gift from a young man who died leaving it to my mom and us. I initially only wanted to see this house, but we knew how much the young man had always wanted to fix it up for his mother, who was my mom's best friend. We kept this home, fixing it up little by little over 12 years, with my mom passing away in 2013. I applied the inheritance money from the sale of her home to the remodeling of that Granada Hills home where I still reside.

By 2016, Ted required dialysis three times weekly. He opted to have peritoneal dialysis initially, probably thinking it would be easier to do at home with my assistance. This was shortlasting because Ted never met the requirements to do it for himself. He had one home emergency incident then visited the kidney dialysis center three times weekly.

Ted did well on the treatment and was able to maintain his daily self-care. He relied on me for doctor visits and managing his overall healthcare, which I did faithfully. I had taken care of my mom's friend's son for 3 and a half years, next my mom for 10 months, and now Ted for a 6-year duration.

We learn many lessons as we get older. When my sister discovered she had breast cancer, as had our mom, she elected to go ahead and have a double mastectomy in October 2021. I was rushing to go to Las Vegas to be with her when I fell, breaking my back in three places with severe compression fractures at L2, L4 and L5. I was rushed to the hospital by ambulance after a neighbor heard me screaming. I was soon fitted with a full-body brace and had to learn how to walk all over again in a rehab center.

A nurse neighbor and other visiting nurses regularly checked on Ted as I recovered. Everything was pre-arranged for Ted to receive dialysis in Las Vegas, so after I was discharged from rehab, we were driven to Las Vegas to help care for my sister. A friend offered to drive us home for Christmas that year, since neither Ted nor I could yet drive. We did get home and fully unpacked, having what would become Ted's and my last Christmas together.

The day after Christmas, Ted said he did not want to go to church, so I prepared a nice dinner for when he woke up. He went into the bathroom when I called him for dinner and he was too weak to help himself up. I tried several times to pull him up but could not. I immediately called the fire department, and they transported him to the nearest hospital.

Because of Covid precautions, I was not allowed into the hospital. I waited for a call and was informed Ted had Covid and pneumonia. He eventually got better and was moved to the local rehab center where I had been. I believed he would get good care there and would be transported to his regular dialysis center. I was not allowed to visit at the rehab either, so I went to the dialysis center three times weekly to get out of my car in the open air and quickly see Ted. He knew I would figure out some way, and this I did.

All the things I had routinely assisted Ted with as needed, I was no longer doing. Thoughts of losing him flashed before me frequently—thoughts about what we both could have done differently to love God more and love one another more.

Ted relapsed and was tranferred back to the main hospital. At one point I received a phone call letting me know that he was not eating and would need a feeding tube inserted. I said, "No, please tell him Linda said to eat, and he will eat." Ted had a hearing problem and was not being talked to loudly enough. Once this was addressed, this same doctor called me back to say, "You were right. He just finished 90 percent of his meal."

Ted required assistance to turn him in bed, but was transferred again to begin his rehab care. There were no vacant beds at the previous rehab, so he was sent to a facility I didn't like. I never received updates on Ted's care there, even though I left numerous messages. One day the attending physician returned my call to let me know he would phone after seeing my husbnad. He did, but to inform me he had found Ted unconcious. My husband was being moved to the emergency room.

I rushed to the ER but was not allowed inside. Somehow I received God's favor and was let in by the woman who admitted me when I broke my back. I found Ted diaphoretic with a fever over 102 degrees and in a state of unconciousness. "Ted," I said. "Squeeze my hand if you hear me." He squeezed my hand, as if he truly was grateful for every day each of us had with one another in our 45 years of marriage.

Wherever did we go wrong? I was losing my friend whom I had spent forever wanting to be my very best frined. Seldom did Ted ever tell me, "I love you," and I would always try to understand him better, no matter what. He was a man of few words with a quiet mannerism. A serious heart and quirky sense of humor as well.

When the three nurses came in to reposition Ted, I could see sepsis had set in and evidence that Ted had been neglected. I felt so helpless. They admitted Ted on the oncology floor for comfort care measures. The hospital Chaplain came to speak with me. My son was allowed to go upstairs with me, and Ted's daughter was on her way to be with us too. We were met by a male nurse named Angel who was wonderful. I let him know I wanted to particpate in all of Ted's needed care, which I was allowed to do until he died at 7:15 the next evening.

I never left Ted's side, and sang some favorite songs to comfort us both in his transition into the arms of Jesus. I had believed Ted would live another couple of years, pre-Covid, because his foot had been healing so well prior to that. It was Angel again who was with me shortly after Ted's passing. This for me was the biggest marker that served to remind me of how we are all travelers on a pilgrimage to meet Jesus, and we only have one life to live in excellence.

♦ Rev. Linda Housden

This photo was taken outside my husband's hospital room with Nurse Angel, shortly after my husband passed. I cherish this photo, because it truly was as if this was this was the very last message that Ted wanted for me to have in my heart forever, said to me directly from him. Ted believed in me 100% and also knew how coloring other peoples lives was who I am, and the person that he married. I had not noticed this huge mural right outside his door, but God's big kinda love never fails and at the time of Ted's passing little did I know I would be writing in this book Scars to Stars. God wants for us all to remember how BIG his love is as we fullfill the Great Commission in our lives.

God allowed me to learn many lessons on my journey together with Ted. There is power in transparency, and it often is through our words that provide the ability to heal, comfort, and help someone else who may feel like they are all alone on their journey. I was never alone because God was always there for me, as He is today and each and every day.

In dealing with a workaholic marital partner, I would face things differently than I did... with less resentment and a greater measure of understanding. These are 10 tips I can share:

- Enjoy the time you do have with one another, making fewer demands and complaints.
- Discuss feelings way more and decide solutions together.
- Avoid negative talk as much as possible.

- Appreciate your spouse's work ethic more and learn how to work through those habits to be able to speak life into every situation.

- Attempt to understand why, even when your spouse is not at work, how they become distracted.

- Better accept your spouse's need to be an excellent provider, which often is conditioned by having a workaholic father. In my situation my husband had to pick peaches and walnuts even as a little boy to help his family to earn money.

- Accept circumstances more readily, and fuss way less.

- Continue focusing on a desire to make good memories.

- Obtain professional help if needed and, if possible, together, which provides additional win-win strategies.

- Practice date nights and short getaways with added vacations placed on a calendar that you plan together.

In closing, marriage requires hard work and learning together what works best. Most often it is the issue of effective communication and an unwillingness to make the decision to go where the peace is at. This requires a change in mindset. I had a better marriage in some ways than I ever realized, and our children had a better dad than they ever got close enough to know.

The two wonder drugs of marriage are self-awareness and self-responsibility, leaning on the power of faith. The kind of war stories that I have shared are perhaps needed more than ever to give younger generations hope. For me, divorce was never an option because I never wanted my first divorce from my son's father either. I believed the scripture verse in Galations 6:9 in my second marriage, selectively bringing in a small circle of friends to pray. Each of these trusted people wanted our marriage to survive and prosper. Against all odds we made it through, often standing on the Word of God.

Galatians 6:9: "Let us not become weary in doing good, for in due season we will reap a harvest of blessings if we do not give up."

Rev. Linda A. Housden, R.N.

"Servant of God, Lovely Linda"

"God desires a surrendered heart"

"But without faith it is impossible to please him: for he that cometh to God must believe that He is, and that He is a rewarder of them that diligently seek Him." —Hebrews 11:6

Reverend Linda Housden, R.N. is often called "Lovely Linda" or "Mother Theresa" of this generation. Her measure of compassion impacts lives forevermore. She learned many life's best lessons while working as a first responder on the Los Angeles Mayor's Crisis Response Team, providing immediate crisis intervention, emotional support, and referrals to families affected by traumatic events. These events were callouts to homicides, suicides, traffic fatalities, SIDS deaths, domestic violence, officer-involved shootings, natural deaths, and in addition, mass casualty events.

Linda's career as a flight nurse, Pediatric/NICU nurse, and American Red Cross Disaster Health Services Supervisor opened up many doors to utilize her practical and professional skills to become a foster parent to 22 special needs infants, do prison ministry, and travel extensively to many countries on short-term missionary teams for a period of 10 years.

Today, Linda is a certified Life Coach, entrepreneur, and public relations director for the company of Ijascode, a global incentivized digital marketing company. She was a co-author in the books, *Living God's Best Life*, and *From Broken Pieces to Masterpieces*, with Dr. Angella Palmer Banks, Xcellence Inc. She is also the Chief Community Liason for Xcellence Inc., counting it all joy to serve in this capacity as a connector to others, both nationally and globally. Another co-author book project done was with Life On Fire Mentors Nick & Megan Unsworth, and keynote international speaker, James Malinchak, called, *Live Abundantly*. Top thought-leaders shared their secrets for living an extraordinary life, which is possible to have, as we surrender our hearts to God's heart.

My Blurred Opinion

Timothy "T. J." West

AT AGE FOUR, I WAS A VERY HAPPY CHILD. I loved Ninja Turtles and cars—not just Hot Wheels, but actual cars. I knew the makes and models by their emblem and the body shape. The irony is that I ended up losing my sight later that year due to a condition called Steven Johnson Syndrome. I would never learn to drive.

SJS is caused by an allergic reaction to medication, in my case, vancomycin and amoxicillin, taken for an ear infection that could have caused me to go deaf. The effects from SJS vary, but usually start with blistering of the skin. The damage comes later, but your nails and your teeth and basically everything falls out.

It took four and a half months in the hospital with feeding tubes and skin grafts to heal the affected area by pressing Bacitracin ointment onto the body. Then they wrapped me up like a mummy to heal the wound and eventually grow back the skin. It did work but they had to do it multiple times a day.

Everything was excruciating. Think of it like a thousand times worse than a sunburn. You can't touch the area. Every sensation is exacerbated.

I was five years old by the time I got to leave the hospital, though still undergoing many eye procedures. They took skin and cells from a dead person's eyes and from my mother's eye. There were many different surgeries, and one actually ended up messing up my left eye permanently. Technology was so different back then.

As a child, I lived in a small Pennsylvania town called Williamsport. Philadelphia was the closest place with proper hospitals and a burn center. They treated me exactly as if I was a burn victim because of the lack of skin. My mom ended up meeting a guy who was a security guard at that hospital and we ended up moving to Philadelphia.

When I later went to school, my mother told me, "Listen to the adults." Unfortunately that advice didn't benefit me. I was molested by a nurse in school. I was bullied not only by students but also by teachers who refused to let me go to the bathroom. I had to sit in my own mess, which became a huge lawsuit. Also a lot of kids would throw stuff at me, spit on me, kick me...

> *It took four and a half months with skin grafts and feeding tubes to heal the affected area.*

It did get better over the years. Once I got to sixth, seventh, and eighth grades, I started to figure out a little bit of who I was. I began to dress nicer then, but for a while I didn't even want to wipe my own behind. I just felt so violated and distraught as a person. I already had PTSD—though as a kid, you don't know what any of that stuff is.

Teachers told me that because I was visually impaired, I could only go to one particular school—Overbrook School for the Blind. It's in Philadelphia and there's nothing wrong with that school, but it's where they send a lot of impaired kids who don't have bigger dreams.

A few people actually believed in me back then and felt I had potential. So many teachers told me I was kind of useless, though, so that's what I believed instead.

Thankfully, a woman I'm still close with today got me into one of the better high schools. Even though I didn't have the grades, she had built rapport with the principal and higher ups at the school. She had previously brought in other "misfits" who ended up becoming something through that school, so she had credibility and got me admitted there.

Another teacher, a resource teacher who unfortunately just passed away, looked after me. She and I butted heads at the time because I was on a road of self-destruction then. I just didn't care. I didn't want to do anything. I didn't want to apply myself. I was so caught up in believing I was as useless as everyone else told me.

The turning point was when I was failing so bad I would have to go to summer school. I don't know what clicked, but then I started hustling, and I ended up getting through the year. The next few years I was one of the tops kids in the school.

> I was so caught up in believing I was as useless as everyone else told me.

That's when I started to understand depression. Even though my own anxiety and depression weren't necessarily related to my eyesight anymore, I still didn't have my own identity. I wanted credit for trying, and I needed friends. I just kind of went along with what other people liked. If someone said I was a nerd for liking Yu-Gi-Oh cards, I replied, "No, I just play because my friend likes it." Truth is, I loved it, and I spent a lot of money on it.

Even though I actually did well in high school, I sabotaged myself from getting into a really good college. I was so petrified. Maybe I was afraid of success, or of being a failure. I had the grades to get into most colleges. Maybe not Harvard, but decent colleges. Instead I ended up going to the Community College of Philadelphia. It is a good school, but still I didn't apply myself enough.

Eventually I dropped out because I was really sad and lonely. I'd lost my best friend. She died of heart failure. I was in a place where I didn't want to live anymore. In fact, there was a five-year span when the only reason I stayed alive was so my mother and my grandmother didn't have to see me dead. That's not a great reason to live, but at least it's something.

Once, I attempted to kill myself by finding my mother's gun, but it had a lock on it and I couldn't use it. I'm relieved now, but at the time I was really frustrated.

I was so afraid all the time. I didn't apply myself to things. I wouldn't make the extra effort. Sure, I could go out in the street where I lived in Philadelphia and get drugs. But because I was still dealing with PTSD, I was petrified to leave my house unless my mother or a friend or somebody was with me. I was not a very mobile person. I couldn't encourage myself to do much, so for a long time, I was just a shell of a person.

Who I am today developed over time. As a child I never really had an identity. Somewhere along the way I just kept getting through the negative thoughts. But even in the darkest places you can still find some really beautiful things. I would help people here and there—some special needs children, for example. Then someone asked me, "What do you want to do with your life?" I always said, "I want to help people. Or animals." That's just who I was.

There was a period of time earlier where if I saw anybody with happiness, I wanted to ruin it. I didn't want anyone else to be happy because I wasn't happy. A lot of things felt unfair and unjust. Eventually my mom and I reached a point where she said I could move with her and her new boyfriend, or I could go my own way. Although my mom is a very dedicated and loving mother who helped get me through my hardest times, she was trying to give me tough love when I didn't need it. My mental health was spiraling down again and so I moved away, back to the town where I was born. Once there, I got a job, then later got my own apartment and a year and a half or two years later I started working at the place where I'm still working now eight years later.

If I saw anybody with happiness, I wanted to ruin it.

This place hires people with disabilities. It's something I'm trying to help change while I'm there. I've never liked how people with disabilities are treated differently. I never was a leader, and I never wanted to be. In fact, I'd hide from any kind of leadership, but when I got there, I realized we weren't treated as individuals. They made us like one singular entity—visually impaired people, or blind people. That bugged me.

It lit a fire under me. I heard someone suggest starting a podcast about me and what I went through. Mental health has plagued me my whole life, and when I look out in the media, I don't think it's talked about beyond a very surface level. So I started doing just that, and also interviewed a few of my friends.

In my research I realized that people with disabilities who blog or do any kind of entertainment tend to stick to the body part they know. In my case, it would be visual impairment. But sticking to the eye department also bugged me. I wanted people to see the bigger picture. I wanted others to understand how amazing people with disabilities are, and how strong we are, and how much we've overcome after what's been thrown on our plate.

> *Mental health has plagued me my whole life.*

So I started interviewing people from all over the world. From the United States to South Africa and many places in between, we talk about subjects like addiction and domestic violence, things I never experienced firsthand. Because of those discussions, I finally started to share about being bullied and about being molested. The first time, it was very draining, as I had to mentally relive the awful stuff. But now I can say it without any shame whatsoever. It doesn't bother me now because I know I'm doing my best to help other people. It's become this beautiful thing I never envisioned.

It grows a little every year and it's something I'm very proud of. When people ask me the name of the podcast, I mention that people with disabilities often have a very dark sense of humor. The podcast is called My Blurred Opinion. It's a play on own my disability, yes, but I know so many people with sight who are mentally blind. Their opinions are also a little blurred.

Sometimes a disability is the biggest gift. The visually impaired can see what other people can't. We're less likely to be biased. We have real empathy for others, and we're often less judgmental. I'm not saying there aren't people with disabilities who are racist or sexist, but generally they are more open-minded, even with a lack of experience. Maybe they've never been around a black person or a gay person, but because they know what it's like to be judged, they can relate. We have to start to break the chain somewhere. There are good qualities even in bad people.

Me and my father have never been very close. I wanted to do something more therapeutic because I'm trying to build or heal relationships that are worth healing. My father wasn't always the greatest father but he wasn't the worst father either. He never beat me, never physically abused me. He mentally abused me sometimes though as he was an alcoholic and had rage issues. But I'm proud of him because he's going to classes for that. He is becoming a better person. He does have a lot of health issues, and when some people ask me about Karma, I don't think he deserves that. I don't wish any kind of ill on anyone. Some say we should just get rid of the horrible people altogether, but I don't wish people to have heart problems or trouble walking.

I thought it was a great episode because there was no conflict. It just flowed. I wanted to show that I have a new established relationship with my father, because a lot of people don't get to make amends with a parent who wasn't the greatest. Maybe they die after something unspeakable happens and you just can't heal. Sometimes there are people sitting around wanting to heal but they just don't have it in them. Maybe my podcast could help them.

A friend and I did back-to-back episodes, one with her, and one with her fiancé. His spoke strictly about mental health and how it affected and had plagued his life, while her interview was about having a really bad stroke. In the hospital, her mother stayed by her side the whole time. While she was unconscious, she could hear things but couldn't move any part of her body. The doctors were saying that she wasn't going to wake up and she was never going to live a great life.

She now has her own company which she calls Pinky Moves, because at one point she started to move her pinky and her mother saw it. Even though the doctors kept telling her mother there was nothing they could do and she was just a vegetable, her mother stayed and watched. At one point, she says her mother yelled, "Please, just move your pinky one more time," and got all the doctors into the room. This woman did everything in her power to move that pinky, and she did. Finally the doctors got her the help she needed, but even when she started to talk a little bit again, and even when she finally started to walk again, they still kept saying, "This is as good as it's going to get." Today she's a powerful speaker!

She walks and talks with about 90-95 percent function in every area.

Through the podcast, I've talked to Ashton Kutcher's twin brother because he has cerebral palsy, and I've talked to some athletes and celebrities. Talking about mental health and suicide prevention is something I'm really passionate about and now I get to do it all the time.

I did a presentation for a group down here because a kid killed himself in our high school. It's so unfortunate. It seems like every celebrity that dies nowadays is from suicide. There's no bias on age, but honestly, it seems like the youth is getting hit the worst.

As a person who was suicidal for a long time, it's rough and I have to help a few people off the ledge. My mom's best friend killed herself, and I knew a few people who have killed themselves. It's terrible even if you weren't really close to the person.

One of the travesties is how we're hardly allowed to say the word "suicide" or the phrase "sexual assault" anymore. Instead, we have to say, "SA," but who's actually going to say, "I got SA'd"? It takes away from the feeling of how awful it is. One time when I posted something about suicide prevention, Facebook blocked me even though all I was trying to do was help people. I'm careful about what I post now. We really try to talk about mental health and specific diagnoses that people can relate to without being explicit around suicide.

I could get on the podcast and talk about me and my cat the whole time, but I don't. Or I could just talk about visual impairment and blindness, or about mental health, but I don't. I'm trying to show the bigger picture, by interviewing people who are deaf or homeless or other things I've never experienced. I can't personally help someone feel less alone who's suffering with something I've never experienced, but through interviewing all kinds of people on the podcast, it's a way to make a bigger difference for those people through creating community.

I interviewed one guy who was healing from porn addiction. At first I wondered if I should do it, but then realized I didn't need to judge his story over anyone else's. It's an addiction. It's something people do suffer from. At the end of the day, we're in a sexual society. Porn affects people in different ways, and there might be someone out there right now who feels like they're just an awful person because they have this problem. So here was this guy saying, "Look, I went through it, and I don't have that problem anymore."

I do believe mental health is also a disability though some argue that. There are certainly a lot of people in wheelchairs who will tell you that the most crippling part about their disability is the mental health that comes with it. There have been times when I wanted to say, "Screw this. I'd rather lose the rest of my sight than deal with whatever..." Of course I don't want to lose my sight at all, but a lot of times when you hear me talk about the issues I've gone through, I don't even get to the eyes.

> *I do believe mental health is also a disability.*

It's about how people show up in the world, and it's also about what we deal with on a daily basis based on what other people think of our disability. There are so many who live with chronic pain, and others don't even believe them because it's an internal symptom. I have a little chronic pain myself, but nothing in comparison to someone with fibromyalgia or Multiple Sclerosis.

We use the expression, "Put yourself in someone else's shoes," but it's impossible to ever completely understand what any other human deals with on a daily basis. I know plenty of people who are missing limbs who say, "Thank God I'm not visually impaired," and I look at them the same way. I say, "Are you kidding me? I'm happy I have my arms and legs." It's just a matter of perspective and life experiences.

I've come to realize that all disabilities are terrible, but people with disabilities can still make good things happen. If it wasn't for everything that happened to me, I don't know what kind of person I would have become. Still, I don't love it and I wouldn't wish it on anybody, but it's made me care more about maintaining what I have.

What we need more of is community. We're supposed to look out for each other. It's not a one-way thing. Forget all the biases and ignorance, and just go out and support each other. Anything that has changed for the good in this world has been done together.

We're so divided. Forget white and black, or men and women. My goal is whatever I can do to make it better for everyone. Judith Heumann was a huge figure in the disability community who died earlier this year. If I could do even a fraction of what she did, I will be happy. I'm just trying to put a little bit of good energy into this world... because we sure as hell need it.

Timothy "T. J." West

T. J. WEST has lived with an eyesight disability from a very young age. He is a kind and giving human that is a pleasure to know. He started the podcast "My Blurred Opinion" with the message of giving a voice to those who don't have one....

Podcast: My Blurred Opinion

Facebook: facebook.com/tj.west.96

Instagram: @tjssafespaceforall

A Tale of Two Cousins

Chad Gaines

EVERY YEAR IN AMERICA, more than 8,000,000 people suffer from trauma and PTSD. Most live with this nightmare in silence.

Let me share two stories with you. One is a tale of darkness that was turned into light. The other is also about darkness, but without the light at the end. The thing that distinguishes these two tales is the different mindsets each person had for their future.

Two boys are cousins, four years apart in age. Both lived with alcoholic dads, and at the time, both had mothers in the house while they were growing up. As adults, both did time in prison. The only real difference was that one mother was physically abusive while the other one was not.

I asked myself a series of questions.

- What are the effects from being in an abusive family?
- At what point will these children who have turned into adults now be affected by their abusive childhood?
- What would be impacted by their past?

Those questions would become my drive and my lifelong work to answer. I've come to know thousands of horrific stories. Several ended up in prison, while others involved murder.

Statistics show that 40 percent of children who come from highly physical and abusive childhoods and violent alcoholic families become serial killers in their lifetime.

A Tale of Two Cousins ♦

Back in my thirties, I interviewed both cousins, asking them the same questions, and what I found was shocking.

I asked the older cousin, "Why did you start drinking as an adult?" His response was, "Because my dad was an alcoholic."

When the younger cousin was 32 years old, he gave up alcohol. I asked him, "Why did you stop drinking?" His quick response was, "Because my dad was an alcoholic."

"Why did you start drinking?"

The questions brought out the same response. The clear difference for them was their ways of thinking. Both boys, now men, lacked education. Both had grown up being told they would never amount to anything. Then how is it that the older cousin will not be up for release from prison until February 2047, and the other cousin was left to deal with more physical abuse? In 2001, the younger cousin's stepdad was murdered by his mother.

On my drive from the prison to my home, my mind wandered. How did the older cousin get sentenced to serve 60 years, while the younger cousin endured a stabbing, beatings, a broken nose, being set on fire, and dealing with a murder at the hands of his mother? Even more important, when did the younger cousin start on a different path in life?

My name is Chad Gaines. In the story you read above, I was the younger cousin. I was 28 years old back in 2001, when my mother killed my stepdad in a small farm town in Northern Indiana. For me, it was about survival and out-living her.

In 2004, I was honored as one of the Ten Most Outstanding Young Americans in the country. In 2023, I wrote a book about my story, *WHO AM I (The Chad Gaines Story)*, and it became a best seller. They are now turning my book into a major motion picture about my life. I don't speak about those things to boast. I'm telling you to help you understand that if you're still breathing, you have a chance to do great things. There is a way out for you.

When something horrific happens to you... suddenly you have no choice but to live in a world you don't recognize anymore. Inside the violence of the mind, you can't escape. It feels dark even when it's daylight. You feel lonely even when you are surrounded by people. Only existing. Unsure of your identity.

> "Because my dad was an alcoholic."

You can see life going on right in front of you. You even try to reach out and touch that world. But you can't. Yet. Or ever.

There are people out there who are just living their mundane lives and seem to not have a care in the world. You may sometimes try to live in that world, too. At least briefly. This involves fake smiles and pretend interest in small talk. It's exhausting. So you choose to isolate instead. That felt much safer to me than being with people who didn't understand how my mother was just footsteps behind me. Always.

"I'll fucking kill you, you little son of a bitch." Those words still play in my mind over and over, thousands of times a day!

It would be nice to switch places with those other people… to not have such a loss constantly replaying in your mind. All those anxious thoughts ruminating. It's a rude awakening when everyone else just keeps moving. Laughing. Making plans. While you are suspended in time. A time you will never escape from.

I was just going through the motions seven days a week. I had pain so deep that I can't even exactly pinpoint where it was coming from or when it started. It was invisible to others on most days. But it was always there. And it always hurt. It chases me, like my mother once did all those years ago.

People will say they are "always with you."

But where? It feels so long since you have heard their voice say anything. Most days it almost feels like you have been abandoned to roam this unrecognizable world alone. And on the other end, you find yourself feeling guilty for trying to move forward without them.

Loss works this way. It's a big ball of tangled up feelings—somewhere between that crust in your eyes and a fishhook in your big toe. And it takes as long as it takes to move through these confusing emotions.

It takes patience, lots of self-care, and being kind to yourself. Mostly it takes self-control, which I lack on most days, because grief is a lonely journey where you are the only one who truly understands how this trauma feels.

As a life coach now to many who are dealing with the long-term effects of trauma and PTSD, I can tell you that the more I speak on stages around the United States, the more my story is opening countless other adults to share their own stories to help the healing. Let me tell you how this has affected my life.

Long after my mother's death back in 2017, I still carry the horrific flashbacks. We lived in a farm town in Indiana in the 1980s. I never really experienced anything other than violence in my childhood. However, as a 50-year-old dad and husband, I can tell you what it's like to dive two stories off a boat into the Pacific Ocean off the coast of Honolulu. I can tell you what it's like to walk onto a movie set with the excitement that comes with it. I can also tell you what it's like to feel small and less than zero on some days when I wake up.

I can tell you what it's like to walk on to a movie set...

All through life we will encounter grief, shortcomings, heartbreak, and small victories. It's called life, and we can't get out of it alive. I think when I first became aware of my memory loss was somewhere between 2018-2019. During times at work, I caught myself writing down simple drink orders so I wouldn't forget during the 50 seconds it took me to get to the soda machine.

As time went forward, I found myself losing my balance and running into tables that would lead to big leg bruises. By the spring of 2018, I would forget lines of a book I was reading. Even people that I'd worked with every day for a few years, I would lose their names somewhere in my brain. I would then spend hours focusing on reading their name tags to remember some of my friends. My brain wouldn't process conversations I had with guests at work. It got so bad that I left my keys in my post office box more than eight times. I dismissed it as "I'm just getting older, I guess."

For me, I believe 2020 opened the flood gates to how this was affecting my mental health. After being laid off from COVID, I became isolated from nearly everyone. I didn't want to go out or talk to people. I didn't know how to explain it—how I was a public speaker, but that light was losing its brightness.

I started listening to music for about 14 hours a day to fight off what I was hearing in my head. I wasn't able to sleep at night. I could only get to sleep when it became daylight outside my window. I made 12 trips across the country and back that year, but I could barely tell you about three of them.

That's when I realized that I needed to write my story before I forgot everything about my life and everyone I knew. I have met a lot of wonderful talented people throughout the world. I wanted to tell them how much I appreciated them coming and going in my life.

It took me nearly six years to write my book. One lady told me, "It didn't take you six years to write your story." She said, "It took you fifty years to write your life story." I cried a lot while writing in the middle of the night. I wrote about what it was like after my dad left our home in 1979. The beatings, stabbing, and alcohol abuse as a young boy and teen. I also went into detail about how my mother killed my stepdad in 2001.

> *I can also tell you what it's like to feel small and less than zero.*

It was very disturbing to write about my mother killing people. I was embarrassed and full of guilt. It only just began with my stepdad. After my mother moved in with my grandmother, that's when everything changed, and people started to die inside of their home. I had quite a few reasons to give up and put a gun to my head and pull the trigger. Fear did take control of me many times. The embarrassment made me feel I would never amount to anything.

I found it's best to control those triggers by having a daily routine for everything! I have a wonderful wife who studies daily to understand my thoughts, feelings, and the effects of my Complex-PTSD. On stage, I explain that life is like the sport of football. It's about blocking and tackling—blocking out your fears and tackling the opportunities. These skills can be applied to anyone's life.

I share the same message with middle and high school students. Life is going to hurt! In fact, it's going to uppercut some of you right in the mouth. I give it to them straight because they deserve to know.

The wonderful people I get to work with or share a stage with are the same people my mother once told me I would never meet. When I came across this book series, *Scars to Stars*, I honestly felt it was written for me. The impact of these stories here inspires me to continue with my work worldwide.

Chad Gaines

CHAD RICHARD GAINES was born on June 3, 1973. An author and speaker now, he is widely known for his book, *Who Am I*, and the details of his horrific child abuse when he was a young boy. He spends much of his time lecturing and coaching on PTSD and its long-term effects. Gaines is now a coach about the concepts of resilience. In 2001, his mother killed his stepfather, and he writes the details in his book based on his life. In 2004, Chad Gaines was honored as one of the Ten Most Outstanding Young Americans (TOYA) in the country. In 2008, Gaines was honored with the Daily Points of Light by President of the United States, George Bush.

In 2020, Hollywood writer Stevie Long wrote the movie script based on Gaines' life. Filming of the movie *Pocket of Hope (The Chad Gaines story)* is taking place in San Francisco this summer. Additionally, Chad has appeared on many podcasts worldwide, sharing his story and message... "Keep getting back up..."

For more information about Chad Gaines and his programs please visit:

www.gaineschad.com
#thechadgainesstory

Set Apart

Ted McConnell

I AM COMPELLED TO START MY STORY WITH THIS VERSE:

> *"Before I formed you in the womb I knew you, before you were born I set you apart; I appointed you as a prophet to the nations." —Jeremiah 1:5*

Sometime before March 9, 1962, God set me apart, appointed me as a prophet to the nations, and so far for 61 years of this earthly life, kept me from harm and danger, seen and unseen.

My earliest recollection of a life set apart is from the summer of 1966. A lady named Miss Robertson picked me up from the children's home. Think of the scene from *Annie* with all the kids playing together. I remember she had this old black Dodge Comet. I was really into cars at a young age. We took a winding road and then pulled up in front of a big white house. She took me up the stairs to meet the people who would be my foster parents.

I sat across from them at breakfast. They asked if I would like to live with them and showed me what would be my own bedroom with a trundle bed. There was a weeping willow tree in the front yard, and a back yard with another huge tree that rose above the three-story house.

I thought about it. My own room? My own bed? My own front and back yard? My own screened-in porch to look out over the street and watch the cars go by? Compared to being at that crowded children's home—which I recall as full of love—I said yes. Yes to my own room, my own bed, my own house, my own parents. Yes to all of it.

I moved to East Walnut Hills, Cincinnati. I was four at the time, and on my fifth birthday, my parents brought me a black puppy. When asked what I would name him, my parents knew I loved Batman so they suggested I call my new puppy either Batman or Robin. I also loved watching the Green Hornet show, so I decided to name the dog Kato, after the sidekick character.

I had Kato for 14 years before he passed. He was my protector and I was his. One time my mom swung at me with a broom for doing something I probably should not have done. Kato bit her on her leg, which is not funny, but it happened. Another time, my brother jumped on me in the basement. We were playing and wrestling as brothers do. Kato ran over and bit my brother on the jaw. He was the smallest dog on our street, but Kato was the meanest and most protective.

My brother was two years younger than me. We're both fair skinned. We grew up in a large house on a street full of kids with lots of cousins. My mom had six sisters and two brothers, and everyone had kids, so we had a large loving family. The two of us were accepted as family. My mom was one of the oldest of her siblings so that meant I was one of the oldest cousins. Some of them never knew they we were actually adopted into the family until they were age 19, but the love never changed. Till this day, we have get-together dinners, out of town trips, and cousins' reunions.

My brother was brought into this home around two years after me. We shared the room with the trundle bed. I slept on top and he slept on the bottom. There were always renters in the lower half of the three-story house.

We had an air conditioner in our third-floor room because it was so hot there. That made us one of very few kids with air conditioning in their own room. Central air was not available at the time. We were among the first on the street to get a floor model Zenith console television and stereo player, and we each at one time or other had to get up and go change the television channel or adjust the rabbit ear antennas because remote controls and cable television had not been invented yet.

This reminds me of when my first daughter was about 6 and I called her downstairs to bring me the remote which was across the room so I could change the channel. My wife thought it was mean, but I thought it was part of the privilege of being a parent and having a child, though she did not think it was funny.

When my brother and I went to school, we walked to Burnett Elementary on Burdett Avenue. I went to Walter Peoples Junior High school on Erie Avenue, and my brother went to Western Hills on the other side of town. After high school he went off to the service and I attended Wilberforce University.

When my younger friend and I walked home from school one day in sixth grade, we took a shortcut through this old man's yard. He ran out, intoxicated, waving a silver pistol. My friend Clarence took off, but I froze in my tracks, staring at that pistol thinking I would die. When the man finished cursing me out, he told me to go on home. As soon as I got out of the yard and back onto the sidewalk, I saw my friend several blocks down the street, still running. I was angry with him but we ended up laughing... and we never told our parents about that ordeal.

My brother went off to a 20-year military career. He married a beautiful young woman but they had no children until he retired. At age 53 he had his first child, at the same time as I had my first grandchild. Unlike some in the service, my brother was blessed to be around for them.

We grew up in a big house together on a street full of kids. We played baseball on one street and football on another. On yet another we would play kickball or build go-carts out of wheels from old grocery carts. We spent some of our summers building clubhouses. We even built fire pits. I ran track in elementary, played volleyball in junior high school, and had a lot of friends. Life was good.

My mom and dad divorced. Mom had a long-time boyfriend. Although I stayed in touch with my father until he passed (when I was in my 30s), we also had another male figure in our lives. We sang in the church choir together.

I gave my life to Christ at an early age and am now a Deacon and chairman of the Deacon board and joint board. I've served as president of our neighborhood council trustee and also steer a large safety committee. I started an intern program at my job before I worked for the city of Cincinnati. I've also worked with the youth ministry at church since my daughter was age 13. She's now 32.

Because my mom was the oldest of eight siblings, I was one of the older cousins. Some may not even know we were foster kids. One cousin only learned it when he was 19, but he hasn't treated me any different since that day. We are such good cousins that we have reunions even without our parents or aunts or uncles, traveling to each other's homes, from Ohio to California and in between.

When we were kids, when we got home from school, we changed into play clothes. Same on Sundays after church. I still have a closet that's full of church suits, church shoes, and church shirts. I guess everything else is play clothes.

After high school, I went away to Wilberforce University, a historical black college right outside of Xenia, Ohio. That's where I lived with my wife and three beautiful children—daughter Ashley, son Jeremy, and another son Daniel. Their mother and I got married at age 24 and after a 20-year marriage we divorced. But I regret nothing.

Now I have a granddaughter and a grandson by Ashley, another granddaughter and grandson by Jeremy, and my third son is married but has not had children yet. I'm okay with that. All my children are doing well. The youngest has recently moved out West from Atlanta and I plan to visit him this summer.

Personally I am an IT professional and I work for the city of Cincinnati. I chose the tech field later in life, after working in mental health where I got burned out. I thought that with computers I wouldn't have to work with people, but

> *I thought that with computers, I wouldn't have to work with people...*

my mistake was that every computer has a person tied to it. In reality, I doubled my trouble... but I've enjoyed 25-plus years in this field which has great job security.

I love boating, which I've enjoyed for approximately 30 years. There's nothing like being out on the water—like Jesus and his disciples, relaxed at times but hard at work at others. I personally don't fish off my boat but I do invite others to come join me and relax... so I guess that might make me a fisher-of-men.

> ...but my mistake was that every computer has a person tied to it.

I am in a seven-year relationship and plan to marry, possibly this year. She was previously married for 31 years, and has four children. Our blended family already knew each other because we all attended the same church growing up.

One of my female church friends was the one who suggested I ask her out. Her husband passed the same year as my divorce, so it had been nine years for each of us.

If you were to ask me to describe her, I would use Proverbs 31:11–31 which defines a virtuous woman:

Her husband has full confidence in her
    and lacks nothing of value.
12She brings him good, not harm,
    all the days of her life.
13She selects wool and flax
    and works with eager hands.
14She is like the merchant ships,
    bringing her food from afar.
15She gets up while it is still night;
    she provides food for her family
    and portions for her female servants.
16She considers a field and buys it;
    out of her earnings she plants a vineyard.
17She sets about her work vigorously;
    her arms are strong for her tasks.
18She sees that her trading is profitable,
    and her lamp does not go out at night.

¹⁹In her hand she holds the distaff
   and grasps the spindle with her fingers.
²⁰She opens her arms to the poor
   and extends her hands to the needy.
²¹When it snows, she has no fear for her household;
   for all of them are clothed in scarlet.
²²She makes coverings for her bed;
   she is clothed in fine linen and purple.
²³Her husband is respected at the city gate,
   where he takes his seat among the elders of the land.
²⁴She makes linen garments and sells them,
   and supplies the merchants with sashes.
²⁵She is clothed with strength and dignity;
   she can laugh at the days to come.
²⁶She speaks with wisdom,
   and faithful instruction is on her tongue.
²⁷She watches over the affairs of her household
   and does not eat the bread of idleness.
²⁸Her children arise and call her blessed;
   her husband also, and he praises her:
²⁹"Many women do noble things,
   but you surpass them all.
³⁰Charm is deceptive, and beauty is fleeting;
   but a woman who fears the LORD is to be praised.
³¹Honor her for all that her hands have done,
   and let her works bring her praise at the city gate.

I'm not sure if my story fits within the definition of this volume, *Scars to Stars*, because I don't really believe my life was that scarred. Some of my friends have stories of womanizers, drunks, sometimes pimps, or drug-addicted men. My testimony is that God has always had his hand on me so...

I now end my story with this verse:

"For I know the plans I have for you, good boy," declares the Lord. "Plans to prosper you and not harm you, plans to give you hope and a future." —Jeremiah 29:11 (NIV)

I would like to give a shout out to my cousin, Jacquala Shropshire, for making this story possible by asking me to be a co-author in this volume.

I would also like to thank Deana and the Realize Foundation for making this possible by doing all the wonderful work and putting so much of her time, energy, and creativity into this project.

Ted McConnell

I learned as a child that I had a Heavenly Father and I knew that was all I needed. I've seen poverty in the Domminian Republic at age 18 and I never asked my mother for anything after that. I've given away anything that I did not need. I've never had a garage sale. Whatever I gave away was a blessing to me, and it was in condition to be a blessing for the next person. If God does nothing else for me, He has done enough. I've had and have lived a blessed and favored life...

FROM THE CRACK HOUSE TO THE WHITE HOUSE

JACQUALA SHROPSHIRE, PH.D.

I INVITE YOU TO TAKE THIS JOURNEY through some of the darkest moments of my life to a saving grace and mercy on me from my God.

Growing up had moments that scarred me. As a teenage girl my mind disconnected because of experiences of sexual assault and other dark issues. Going to school was difficult, even though I put on a smile and a happy face to hide the pain. I wanted to be like the other kids but I never quite felt like I was.

I wasn't really a social person until I got older. As a child I did everything by myself. It was my way of staying safe. I was independent, and wanted to work, earn money, and try to enjoy life the best I could.

On February 14, 1977, I was baptized in Jesus' name and filled with his Holy Spirit. I attended Zion Temple First Pentecost Church. I had an eagerness to know more about this God. I remember being a junior missionary, but as I grew into a teenager I found myself in not so healthy experiences. My life began to spiral out of control.

My mother took me to court. By the age of 17 I was pregnant with my first child. I spent my pregnancy at a place called Catherine Booth for unwed mothers. They helped me finish school and provided me with parenting skills to help raise my healthy baby boy.

I decided to go into the Army military reserves and my son lived with my mother while I went to boot camp. This was quite an experience. I was already a good athlete so the harsh mental anguish from the drill sergeants was all a big game to me. It was easy to pass their tests.

After basic training for the reserves, my mind just was not where it needed to be. Before long, coworkers introduced me to crack. My life truly spiraled out of control.

This went on for many years, hurting loved ones around me. I remember being in the crack house. There was no God-consciousness. The only thing on my mind was finding the next high.

It seems like yesterday when I finally reached the point where I knew I needed to get away. I hopped on a plane headed to California, desperate for a life change. With $25 in my pocket, I knew that if I could just get away, my change was coming.

Upon arrival I stayed with my cousin and later a friend. It was during this time I landed a job and purchased a raggedy old car. I started going to a church in Los Angeles and that was where my life slowly started to change.

> *With $25 in my pocket, I knew my change was coming.*

Don't get me wrong! I still had struggles along the way. But I wanted to know more about this God who would be able to turn things around. I didn't know how he was going to do it, but I just believed that he was.

What was really strange was that I started purchasing books pertaining to spiritual understanding and Bible reference books. I was never a great learner, but something in me so strong wanted to learn about God's word that I later became a Sunday School teacher.

It seems odd to become a teacher since I'd kept to myself as a child and was always quiet. But after I began studying, before you know it, I had all kind of books and felt like I was overflowing. As I grew in the things of God, I knew where he was leading me.

Willing to serve with my whole heart, I answered the call to ministry. I began seminary while at Bethany Church in Los Angeles. I can say that I was delivered from crack cocaine without any support or intervention. It was only the Holy Spirit. It took a lot of self-coaching, though, rehearsing God's word back to me. I had to learn all over again that I was his child and he had greater love for me.

I pray for you, my reader, that something has been said to touch your heart, mind, and spirit to let you know you are not alone. If this story helps you to overcome any obstacle, then my labor of love through so many challenges has not been in vain. The enemy tells us that he comes to kill, steal, and destroy—that's his agenda every day.

> *Know that you are not alone.*

It's amazing to me that many people perhaps have gone through similar life experiences to mine and have gone insane or even died. I am blessed today because I am still here to tell the story. My life is so much better now, but that doesn't mean I am living without struggle.

I continued my schooling and was honored with a doctorate from Next Dimension University. I have since gone on five years doing radio ministry on 99ThreeFM. You can find links to listen at http://LetsTalkKingdom.com.

At times I still struggle with my learning and sometimes I feel like things are more than I can handle. But the word of God is awesome. The more I read God's word, it just keeps reflecting back to me that I am who he says that I am.

The Holy Spirit has taught me so much. It's more than just going to church on Sunday morning. We have to be filled with the Holy Spirit in order to live a life that is holy and acceptable unto God. The Holy Spirit helps us on a daily basis to live the life of the scriptures that pertain to righteous holy living. This does not mean we will not make mistakes, because we will. But when we do, we repent and ask for forgiveness.

Like the scripture says, we should be transformed by the renewing of our minds through God's word. This is the transformation that we long to seek daily. I cannot stress this enough. When you and I pray, we need to ask the father God that his will be done in our lives daily.

Let's take a moment and talk about what it really means to pray. Our prayer life should not always be about *having* things, but more about the father's will being done in our lives. Our prayer life should be on behalf of other people and situations that need God's help—standing in the gap for others who cannot pray for themselves. The father uses us to make a difference day by day.

I remember being at a women's conference at lunch time. It was so crowded and I was trying to find seating. As I approached a table, I knew no one there, but I asked if I could take the empty seat. They said yes. The moment I sat down, one of the ladies said to me, "I don't know you, but I know you are a prayer warrior. I would like to get to know you, because I would like for you to come and pray with us at CBS Studios on a monthly basis during our service." This was such a blessing for me—and yes, I was a prayer warrior, and still am. I served that ministry for five years and saw many miracles.

> "I don't know you, but I know you are a prayer warrior."

These were just a few awesome moments in my life that God chose for me where I could make a huge difference in understanding who I was in him.

I want to just share some encouraging words to you right now. Trust God. Trust God with your whole heart, mind, and spirit. Don't try to figure out how it's going to be done. Just know *it will be done*. We serve a God who cannot lie. He has left us a Bible full of promises.

As I continue to develop in the things of God, he has surrounded me with people who helped reshape my character as well as taught me how to become an entrepreneur and an overall better person and woman of God.

I began to work for the state of California as an independent contractor and I have been doing so now for over 30 years. God never ceases to amaze me. Seek him with your whole heart. Please understand, my friend, that problems never stop. But he helps you know better how to handle your mountain when it appears. Faith is the key to unlock all doors.

I am a proud mother and grandmother and an auntie. I am also a mother-in-law to a beautiful woman, inside and out, who married my son. It is precious moments like these when I appreciate life and am grateful that God spared me. I have dedicated my life to serving others and my God.

Let's do some thinking together for a minute. We all remember someone who is no longer here who had struggles. Some have died by suicide and others took an overdose. Still others perhaps were the victim of murder or are even serving a life sentence behind bars. Do we miss them? Yes. If only we could hug them one more time and let them know how much we love them.

I don't know why you picked up this book, but God had a plan for you. He knew there was something in this book that you needed right now in this moment. God is perfect in all his ways. Yes, perfect. He never makes a mistake. You can trust him with your life.

I'd like to pray together.

> Father God, in the name of Jesus I come before you right now with this individual who is reading this book. This didn't happen by accident. You have purpose, and in everything that you do, nothing happens by accident.
>
> I pray strength for this individual right now. I pray wholeness for this individual. And I ask, Lord God, that you extend mercy and grace for this individual right now.
>
> Whatever the mountain this person is facing, give them the strength and grace to climb. Through their faith, they will win and overcome.
>
> Now father God, in the name of Jesus, wipe away the tears, mend the broken heart, and deliver from all unrighteousness and fill this person with your gift of the Holy Ghost.
>
> In Jesus' name, amen.

Now, let's talk about love. When I was out there in the world, looking for love in all the wrong places, I never felt complete. I was so desperate to be loved and held and comforted. But the more I engaged in my relationship with my God, my Lord and Savior, I felt revived and ready to conquer the world.

I felt better about myself. I felt renewed with strength. I really want to emphasize that you are more than a conqueror. No one can ever take that from you. You will never really truly know love until you experience that with God.

You are your greatest cheerleader. Your emotions will always lie to you. But with faith, you don't need facts. You just need belief. Believe your way through what others struggle against. You are on the mountaintop. Smile.

As I write my story, I know that healing has already begun for me. And I know that healing has begun for you, too. Lift your hands and thank God. He loves us so much that he gave his only begotten son so that you and I can live eternally with him.

Believe your way through what others struggle against.

I thank God for every author in this book who has written and shared their story. We all have a story to share with the world. We are all overcomers. We are all bright stars in the sky.

Perhaps one day you, my dear friend, will take out pen and paper and begin to tell your story. No one can tell your story like you can. Who would've ever thought that I would be a writer?

In 2019, I worked on a Christian film with a producer out of Atlanta. God showed himself strong by using me and fulfilling his will in the earthly Realm. Yes, from the crack house to the white house. What this means is from the dark side of my life to the glorious side!

I'm often asked, "Would I have changed anything?" That answer for me is no. It is through my life experiences that God used me and matured me through my struggles. It is where I gained my greatest strength. Through those life experiences I got to know this true and living God and the Holy Spirit abiding in me. When Jesus died on the cross he covered it all. Through his blood I am a new creature in Christ.

I want to take a moment to share with you the importance of taking care of your mind. Understand and know there will be times of struggle. Please allow yourself to ask the Holy Spirit for guidance in every area of your life every day. We need the Holy Spirit to guide us, to show us, and to minister to our minds, revealing God's word to us, because we cannot begin to walk in holiness without God's holy guidance.

The Holy Spirit wants to help you and minister to you always. So to you, my dear reader, I love you enough to tell you to love all of this. You are God's child and he is our Abba daddy. Our God is no rejecter of persons. What he did for me, he will do for you.

Know that you are always in my prayer. I may never meet you in person or ever know your name, but our God knows who you are and he is calling you by your name. That is love. Wow, that is truly love.

I pray this story has blessed you in so many different ways that you will say yes to our Lord and Savior and that you will serve him all the days of your life, with your whole heart, serving his purpose and will for your life, and that you too will be a blessing to others, and that you will tell your story. Someone is waiting to hear that story, just like someone was waiting on me to tell mine, and that person was you.

> *Someone is waiting to hear your story.*

Trust me when I tell you that when God tells us in his word that he will never leave us nor forsake us, he means just what he says. Perhaps you may have never picked up a Bible before or heard a sermon preached. Get ready because you have a destiny that is going to be fulfilled by God.

Get ready to walk into your purpose. It is going to be an exciting time for you like no other! This is just the beginning! Trust God through the process, and remember to set the standard high for the generations of family who are coming after you. Because you will make it, they will make it too!

JACQUALA SHROPSHIRE, PH.D.

DR. JACQUALA SHROPSHIRE has been serving in ministry since 1977. She was ordained as a minister on September 13, 2015. In August 2019, she received her Doctorate in Theology from Next Dimension University, and her Ph.D. in September 2023.

She is the Founder of Jacquala Shropshire Ministries, in which she is an advocate for God's kingdom, which inspired her to start her own radio show, Let's Talk Kingdom Radio Show. The show is a platform for believers to have diverse conversations about God and his kingdom.

facebook.com/JacqualaMinistries

I would like to personally thank my dearest son Reginald (pop) and my beautiful daughter in love, Erica, and my grandchildren as of this writing, Jakai and Kylie, for their charismatic love and creative thinking outside the box. I credit Dr. Danielle for being the strength of how a family of love should be, as we exhibit the love of Christ daily.

LOVE IS THE GREATEST GIFT IN LIFE:
TO KNOW LOVE IS TO HAVE SELF-LOVE

GEOFF HUDSON-SEARLE

Steve Brunkhorst once said:

> *"As we weave the tapestries of our lives, we gradually begin to see our designs from a wider angle of years. We may or may not be pleased with what we see. Yet, no design–not in the living world–is carved in stone. We have the gift of free will to change our designs as we wish."*

I BELIEVE EVERY SINGLE PERSON ON THE PLANET HAS PASSION, and if directed in the right way it can create amazing things, however passion in the opposite can destroy. Unfulfilled passion creates a cavity between your present and your true potential, which takes away from your ultimate desire and purpose in life.

Growing up, determination and perseverance were a way of life for me. In my first book, *Freedom after the Sharks,* I talk about how each of us is a reflection of the experiences of our lives. However, whether and how we succeed is determined by how we cope with those experiences and what we learn from them.

Despite personal and professional setbacks, everyone has a story and the journey to success is our learnings. We all possess the determination, drive, and skills to create a successful and happy life. The bigger question is whether we choose to use these skills... and if so, do we use them for the greater good?

Change has a funny habit of teaching you much about yourself; it goes to the core of your own weaknesses, strengths, and eccentricities.

There is much discussion around trust, love, and relationships. When we are in love, the world is golden and nothing gets us down. When we are out of love, we are desperate to regain those feelings we had while in love. The desperation can become so intense, we find ourselves thinking and doing things we would be ashamed to tell our best friend.

> *Change has a funny habit of teaching you about yourself.*

The excitement of falling in love, being in love, is not just a thrilling psychological and emotional experience. It is also a bio-chemical experience—what might be called a "high"—with resemblances to a chemical addiction. It also is subject to withdrawal, which becomes evident during a break-up.

Some of the neuro-chemicals in the brain associated with being in and out of love are: dopamine, serotonin, norepinephrine, adrenaline, and phenylethylamine. Depending on the level of these chemicals in the blood, we might be ecstatic or terribly depressed. Research has shown a similarity in blood chemistry and neural activity between people in the infatuation stage of love and those with Obsessive-Compulsive Disorder.

Most people are aware of testosterone and estrogen. These hormones, along with pheromones, are largely responsible for sexual attraction. Pheromones are hormones that are secreted, rather than remaining internal. We often find ourselves attracted to (or repelled by) a person based on their scent. Although pheromones and hormones may ignite the initial spark of a relationship, they aren't able to maintain the relationship. The hormones oxytocin and vasopressin are released in the body during the heights and climax of sexual intercourse and reinforce the attachment and bonding that occurs from physical intimacy.

If a couple were to meet and fall in love, and then take some medication that dampened these love chemicals, they would find themselves rather indifferent about one other. After years or decades of marriage, couples fall out of love due in large part to the waning of these chemicals. One or both partners may seek extra-marital affairs to again feel their thrilling flow. The despair we experience after a break-up is not because we are estranged from our loved one, but because the love chemicals in the blood are no longer there, have diminished, or have vanished. If those same love chemicals could be injected back into the blood, we would feel more than fine.

A solid, stable relationship has a bond of affection based on the initial stages of love. That stable affection can then in turn reignite feelings of lust and romantic love, which reinforce the stable long-term relationship. In many love relationships, it is the initial thrill and excitement that provides most of the interest. When that begins to wane, sexual activity can become more adventurous, which can be a good thing; but it can become overly aggressive and violent as well. The terms "love addiction" or "sex addiction" are appropriate because of the chemical basis of these obsessions. It is not the wild sex or the affair we are after; it is the chemicals that such activities generate.

According to global social media statistics research summary 2022, almost three-quarters of people expect relationship pressures during Christmas, and a poll by charity Relate found that 73 percent of people aged 16 and over in the UK expect something to place pressure on their relationships during the festive season.

The average person uses social media for two hours and 27 minutes every day. That amounts to over five years of your life spent scrolling, posting, and liking. Given that social media has become so ingrained in daily life, it's really no wonder it is now a potential source of tension and conflict in relationships.

The average person uses social media for two hours and 27 minutes every day.

"You won't develop a strong sense of trust if the only time you spend together is sharing TikToks."

It's not all bad news. Social media may positively impact relationships in a number of ways. It's not uncommon to see friends and family post adoring photos of their partner with a lovey-dovey caption to boot. While there are some days when this is the last thing you want to see on your feed, small messages like this projected to a whole network of friends may put a smile on your loved one's face.

It all comes down to being acknowledged, according to Shore Research. "They need to be noticed, they need to know that they matter, and social media can be a wonderful way of doing that in terms of posting small messages, little videos, something that tells that person that they are on your mind and they are on your mind in a very fond way." Still, Shore Research notes that face-to-face communication can't be beaten, concluding, "The reality is this: You can't touch someone over a cell phone."

Real connection is more than just sharing interests. After all, we can talk for over an hour with someone about sports or politics, even if we secretly can't stand them. More profound than mere conversation, true connection can happen without words and with someone we don't even know. On the other hand, constant contact, such as working with someone every day, is no guarantee of actual connection. Connecting with others creates a sense of being open and available to another person, even as you feel they are open and available to you. Other ingredients of human connection are empathy and compassion; we feel goodwill to the person we are connecting with.

Real connection is more than just sharing interests.

Trust is the foundation for love. It's natural over time for feelings of love and connection to fluctuate. Every relationship has emotional dry spells, but trust is consistent and is the foundation that a solid relationship is built on.

Revealing your true self to someone, whether it's your deepest fears or your weird snacking habits, means putting yourself out there. It's not an easy ask of you or your partner, but having a foundation of trust in a relationship does make being vulnerable a little easier. As we get to be our authentic selves, our partner gets to be their authentic selves, and as a result, we get to connect authentically.

Napoleon Hill once said, "Think twice before you speak, because your words and influence will plant the seed of either success or failure in the mind of another."

However, transparent communication can open new doors for us to access a more extensive level of information. When we let go of our individual focus, we are able to experience the dynamics of life to a much greater extent. This allows us to move beyond the interpretation (understanding) of humans as objects in the physical world and thus experience humans from within.

If we recognize that rather than meeting people, we encounter realities in which people emerge, based on what they believe and defend, we develop deeper compassion and understanding. We are aware that in this world we all wear a false smile.

Once we begin to comprehend the inner experiences of others, and to create through our being, we make a quantum leap in our communication. We lift communication up to the next level of evolution. This helps us to acknowledge the true cause of many conflicts, looking beyond the symptoms to the root of the problem.

Have we created a separated culture in society, where we disguise truth and transparency for what people would prefer to hear across technology?

Cultures also differ in how much they encourage individuality and uniqueness versus conformity and interdependence. Individualistic cultures stress self-reliance, decision-making based on individual needs, and the right to a private life.

Having a defined place within a family, a community, and a culture enhances a sense of purpose, stability, and resilience over time. In AI culture, roles are clearly defined and egalitarian. Men and women exist in a cooperative partnership, elders are respected for their wisdom, children are raised to honor adults and to be part of the community as well as the family.

I was discussing with friends recently the morals around an Indian tipi. For more than 400 years, knowledgeable people have agreed that the Indian tipi is absolutely the finest of all moveable shelters. To the Native peoples whose concept of life and religion was deeper and infinitely more unified than his conqueror, the tipi was more. Both home and church, the tipi was a Sacred Being and sharing with family, nature, and Creator. The tipi allowed the Plains Indians to move entire villages to suit the seasons and to be nearer to a good supply of food, wood, and fresh supply for their horses.

When we start to look at relationships, no matter how much time has elapsed or how many relationships have been had, it's hard to truly forget your first love. That person is always going to be special to you, no matter what. It was your first experience with love and the memories stay with you forever.

Falling in love for the first time is a life-changing experience. It can be devastating to have all of that end. If you spend enough time reading advice columns, you notice a pattern. In the stream of sorrows and quandaries and relationship angst, one word bubbles up again and again: First. My first love. My first time. My first ever. And unlike all the relationships that came after, with this one, the past can't seem to stay in the past.

Love is always special, but your first love moves you in a way that is inherently unique. It introduces you to feelings you have never had before, for better or for worse, and is accompanied by a sense of wonder, intrigue, and excitement. Even though your first love may not have lasted, it will be a part of who you are for the rest of your life.

When we think about our first love, there is a mixture of emotions which are hard to explain. But why do many of us still think about it decades later?

We all know someone who got back with their old flame. There's a saying in Spanish, "Where there was fire, ashes remain." It suggests there will always be a special connection between two people who were once in love, and the fire may be rekindled.

But why? Why should one person lodge in our brains any differently, even if other relationships were longer or better? They just weren't quite as intense as the first.

"Where there was fire, ashes remain."

Scientific research on this topic is thin, but collective wisdom among psychologists says it's like skydiving—you remember the first time you jumped out of an airplane more clearly than the tenth time you took the leap.

"Your first experience of something is going to be well remembered, more than later experiences," explains Art Aron, a psychology professor at State University of New York at Stony Brook who specializes in close relationships. "Presumably there'd be more arousal and excitement, especially if it's somewhat scary. And falling in love is somewhat scary—you're afraid you'll be rejected, you're afraid you won't live up to their expectations, afraid they won't live up to yours. Anxiety is a big part of falling in love, especially the first time."

The trust deficit fuels the human experience gap. For all of us who share a zeal to help the world run better and improve people's lives, we can't rest until we bridge that gap.

Spanish essayist Miguel de Unamuno said, "Love is the child of illusion and the parent of disillusion." Is this view cynical or biologically based? Illusions are, by definition, mismatches between physical reality and perception. As with all emotions, love has no external physical reality. It may be driven by neural events, but it is nonetheless a purely subjective experience. So, too, is the wounded heart. Where the arrow enters and exits the heart, there is no heart whatsoever, only an imaginary edge defined by the arrow.

This effect is called an illusory contour. We perceive the shape of the heart only because our brains impose a shape on a very sparse field of data. Neuroscientist Rüdiger von der Heydt and his colleagues at University Hospital Zurich in Switzerland have shown that illusory contours are processed in neurons within an area of the brain called V2, which is devoted to vision. The illusory heart even looks slightly whiter than the background, although it is actually the same shade. Much of our day-to-day experience is made up of analogous feats of filling in the blanks, as we take what we know about the world and use it to imagine what we do not know.

Love is simple when we understand the true meaning of unconditional love—love that transforms and transcends us to a higher level of consciousness. In those moments when we truly love, we become alive, we feel passion, we feel life in every breath. Love is life, at the core of everything we do.

I believe we are not forming unconditional relationships because of our fast-paced, instant access, immediate-response world. We receive things immediately, therefore we expect everything instantly. We have become conditioned to having it all "now." As with the greatest things in life, the magic only happens when things are given time to breathe, when thoughts are clear, when the mind is at peace. It is only in this environment that unconditional love can flourish.

The magic ingredient to unconditional love is finding peace within your own mind; for when your mind is at peace, others will be at peace. It is with this level of peace that bliss exists. Listen to what your relationships are telling you: love and listening go hand in hand.

To love unconditionally you must have the ability to listen to what another person is asking of you—not listening to what your emotions and desires are telling you, but really listening to what that person is asking of you. When we listen to what another requires above our own needs, then we create trust and understanding. When we understand things, the fear goes away. It is only then we can become selfless, allowing the time for love to flourish unconditionally.

We share gifts with loved ones in gorgeous wrapping that makes their hearts leap and their eyes smile. Now think of yourself as the gift inside a beautifully gift-wrapped box. You want to be the best-crafted version of yourself before you share yourself with someone you love—the precious diamond. Imagine what a beautiful life you will live. Give yourself the best chance of healing your heart, which is the key to unlocking everything you desire.

The journey will be fueled with pain, the most harrowing journey you will ever take. But if you listen to love's guidance and wisdom, love will teach you; it will help you to understand yourself so you can understand others better. You owe it to yourself and those around you to follow love; it will teach you how to become the most excellent version of yourself, and what greater gift is there in this world than the ability to give the best version of yourself to those you love?

Love is always there to guide you, protect you, care and comfort you. Love is found in the silence, in the stillness; it will bring you home to who you really are, increasing your self-worth and confidence and allowing your dance to dazzle the world.

For love is simple... if you just listen. Love is the greatest gift in existence.

At different times of our lives, we will need and want different types of relationships. Neither is better nor worse than the other; it is all a personal decision and one that you will feel guided to as long as you follow your heart.

> *Unconditional love transforms and transcends.*

Childhood taught us to value love, but institutions, cities, and technology have taught us to fear commitment. We are trapped in a self-perpetuating cycle of emotional distance.

Most of us really want love, but our actions are at war with this desire. We maintain emotional distance because we fear commitment and rejection, not because that is our true self. We replace the feeling of true intimacy with short-term flings, long-term noncommittal hookups, and sex. We comfort ourselves knowing at least we're not feeling the stinging pain of a broken heart. We have trapped ourselves.

When we keep emotional distance because of the fear of rejection, we lose out on self-love, one of the most important aspects of being human. Deep inside, we know we are unfulfilled but we do not know how to fix ourselves. So, we play a game where there are no winners. We must break free from this damaging culture and learn to love again.

For most, improving relationships is one of the best things we can do. With this realization and committed effort to be more open, honest, and straightforward, I have been able to not only improve how I treat others but also improve the quality of relationships with my circle of wonderful friends.

There's no reason that "love forever" cannot exist. In fact, relationships with so much love and sustainability should exist with the partner that you call your love or spouse. Jo March, author of *Love is Simple,* once said to me, "If love isn't real, you will see the illusion, and when you know that illusion with your eyes closed in the darkness of your mind, you will see with clarity and beauty in the love you experienced and its purpose. It is then when you know that you have let go, and suddenly the light appears, and the eyes are ready to open to the world again, but with a knowing that it wasn't love. It was an experience you needed at that time, a valuable lesson you needed on this journey; it was love sharing a little of itself with you.

"When love is real, your eyes are closed, and you wait, and you wait, and you wait, still in the silence and darkness of your mind. There is no illusion, you just see the darkness, and in the darkness, your heart whispers to your mind that it's there and there to stay. It's there for a lifetime, and it will never go. It is safe to open your eyes to the world. It is safe to see again because you will see with more clarity, beauty, and love. After all, love is now part of you. It came into your heart, took its place, and will never leave; it will be there for eternity because when it's real, it becomes eternal. It is never-ending, and you are changed forever; there is no going back once you genuinely love. I love love, and I feel blessed by love. I am so thankful that love found me, tested me, elated me, and then destroyed me, for it led me on the path to going within and understanding the real love, the best kind of love, the pure unconditional love, the greatest love of all the love that lies inside of you. That is sitting there in every single one of us, waiting to share its secret."

I believe until we truly understand ourselves, we can never really love another person in the way that love wants us to love. For love will give us a glimpse, and there will be many brief and beautiful moments, for it is teasing us, provoking us, showing us what it has the ability to do, and when we have evolved and learned and are ready, it will reveal itself, and you will exist in it for eternity. It will bring peace to your mind and contentment to your soul.

Until we truly understand ourselves, we can never really love another person.

True love is a decision of the will. It's a choice based on many factors, including that "in love" feeling you have for your love or spouse. Such a feeling can be built upon with tenderness, romantic gestures, and caring choices all along the way.

I just know I do not want to be complicit in modern dating culture anymore. I am happy when building real emotional connections in business and in life, and I guess, that is what we all want in the end— to be happy and in love with real connections, real people... a soul connection, not a world stage with actors.

To close, Tamie Dearen, author of *The Best Match,* defines love this way:

> Love is such a small word for what I feel. For the first time in my life, I have a reason to breathe. I'm enchanted with every part of you I know, and I only know a small part so far. I plan to spend the rest of my life searching out every hidden enchantment in your body and soul. And I'm going to cherish and protect you with every fiber of my being. So, do I love you? No... I love love love you.

GEOFF HUDSON-SEARLE

GEOFF HUDSON-SEARLE is a digital non-executive director, serial business advisor, and CSuite executive to growth-phase tech companies, rated by Agilience as a Top 250 Harvard Business School authority covering Strategic Management and Management Consulting.

Geoff has over 30 years of experience in the business and management arena, and is the author of 6 books: *Freedom After the Sharks, Meaningful Conversations, Journeys to Success* vol. 9, *GOD in Business, Purposeful Discussions,* and his latest book *The Trust Paradigm.*

He lectures at business forums, conferences, and universities, and has been the focus of London Live TV, Talk TV, TEDx and RT Europe's business documentary across various thought leadership topics, and has been a regular lead judge at the UK's business premier awards event, The Lloyd's Bank British Business Excellence Awards which is the UK's most prestigious awards program, celebrating the innovation, success, and resilience of British business.

Geoff is a member and fellow of the Institute of Directors, an associate of The International Business Institute of Management, a co-founder and board member of the Neustar International

Security Council (NISC), and a distinguished member of the Advisory Council for The Global Cyber Academy.

He holds a master's degree in business administration and has worked on strategic growth, strategy, operations, finance, international development, growth, and scale-up advisory programs for the British government, Citibank, Kaspersky, BT, and Barclay's among others.

https://ib-em.com/

LinkedIn: @geoffsearle

Blog: FreedomAfterTheSharks.com

Overcoming

Devan Liam Featherstone

I was born on August 6, 1983, the second son of Lynette and John Featherstone, truly the best parents a child could ask for. The abuse, racial hatred, and deceptions they endured never stopped them from being themselves or creating a successful business, nor from being kind and caring and raising three good boys, nor from being a beloved brother and sister, cousin, and friend. They are missed dearly yet endure in my memory. Their words and actions continue to inspire me to overcome the traumas and stigmas that others have sought to brand me with, and to get justice for all those who have suffered at the hand of human traffickers and terrorists.

The first hurdle in my life was the one that stayed with me, and only changed for two reasons. First, I vowed not to pass it to any children I may have. Second, if not for the crimes committed against me, I would have likely been content knowing that who I was and all I could see was enough. My only regret is not being able to see my daughter or son born.

I was born perfect with one exception—a retinoblastoma, a rare form of eye cancer which, if not caught, would have led to my death. The tumorous mass was discovered due to an accident as a baby. While out with my father, I rubbed dog excrement into my eye. But had it not been for this twist of fate, I probably would not have lived to fulfill my destiny.

The information about the dog excrement caused a lot of bullying. Had it not been for friends who never judged me, and loved ones who never saw me as weak, maybe my outlook on life would be different. Knowing that such a small thing could cause harm taught me to open both my mind and my heart to those whose appearances were different. This helped me to help others and bring people together based on similarities, hopes, and dreams.

In this ever maddening world, it is hard to see hope or opportunity, especially after you have been bullied, abused, lied to, abandoned, kidnapped, poisoned, assaulted, trafficked, and left for dead. Nevertheless, all of these things happened to me since I was three years old, on more than one occasion.

In order to heal, I had to recognize that these devastating and disgusting sins were not the hardships which carved my life or molded me. The people who committed these atrocities were deceptive, malicious, and calculated, a weak-minded group of individuals who formulated a plan out of laziness, jealousy, ignorance, hatred, and racism. Their acts culminated in the rape and murder of children, as young as toddlers, as well as human trafficking of myself and other children bombarded by Nazi extremism. I was not to blame for their actions, thus I was not a victim... but that's what they wanted me to feel. Instead, I am a survivor. And more importantly, a protector.

The second hurdle in my life was to realize that the actions taken legally to defend and protect my family, friends, and the people of this world, were not a justification for the attacks. Again, I was not to blame for the assaults that occurred to friends and loved ones. That was an attempt to intimidate and recruit through lies, misinformation, and staged events.

> *I am a survivor. And more importantly, a protector.*

Waking up knowing that people wanted to rape, hurt, steal, and murder my family— because they stole from you, are jealous of you, or are mad at you for criminal decisions they made and the lives they lost—builds up anxiety and animosity, which leads to distrust and rage. While emotionally justifiable given the circumstances, one has to remain calm and act decisively while gathering intelligence, and working through the stress of taking a life in order to protect one.

That stress builds up when you are locked in a cage, after they poisoned you and prodded you with a stick as if you were some junkyard dog. It builds when you are used in child pornography and hate videos to recruit others like them to their cause. It builds when you are humiliated and raped by someone who is now a celebrity. It builds when you have to tolerate those around you who know the truth yet insist the culprit is ethical. The only reason I can bear it all is the comparison of Hitler being a "good general."

I would suggest that in order for you to free yourself from whatever negative mind space you're facing, create a physical timeline of who it is you desire to be. First you'll create the environment you need to become that person. Then you'll take the needed steps to ensure your success, knowing that with every breath and every forward move, you are elevating yourself from the pit of despair you've fallen into—not due to your own faults or flaws, but due to criminal activity, incompetence, negligence, and fear.

We all need someone to talk to.

We all need someone to talk to, to trust, and to rely upon, but we don't always have that luxury after being victimized. It's even harder because you don't want to change who you are, but you also do not want to remain in the same physical, mental, emotional, or spiritual space.

I often wondered if I deserved to be targeted and abused when I chose to stand up to the bullies, the rapists, and the human traffickers. Had I not, would my life be different?

Despite the assaults which left me bloody and beaten, despite the tortures that left me covered in urine, despite being strapped to a pile of burning logs and left to die, despite being drugged and buried alive, despite repeated rapes and attempted humiliations, I know I would choose to stand, again and again, for truth and justice.

The fact is there are some who enjoy hurting people of color and trying to create a sub-class culture, hiding behind others, disguising themselves as normal so they can infiltrate your group and steal from you. They lie to you out of their own realization of inferiority.

I have also experienced firsthand what happens to some immigrants at the hands of those who wear a badge, or who decides his way is best, or the culture has yet to evolve. Whatever is considered "acceptable" behavior in these circumstances becomes the norm and a so-called sign of the times.

Every day becomes an emotional roller coaster. Such stressors cause deep psychological issues. The stress and anxiety then become part of you, manifesting as PTSD, which we all have in our own way.

Don't ever think your problems are too small to matter. If you allow those small bricks to build up, you will soon find yourself trapped in a tomb of despair of your own making. Instead of needing a few kind words, it will take a sledgehammer of therapy, as well as friends and family to help you heal.

> *Don't ever think your problems are too small to matter.*

Mantras are helpful, as are daily affirmations. Ghandi said, "Be the change you seek in the world." Confucius suggested, "If you want a good government, be a good people."

I have traveled the world and seen the best and worst in humanity. I've walked with people through the desert to seek refuge. I've treaded water in the open sea, waiting desperately for rescue, wondering if I, along with those around me, would drown before anyone noticed we were even there. I've helped grown adults to literally keep their heads above water. In itself, this was a harrowing experience, but opening up a cargo container and seeing the bodies of children almost mummified due to heat and time? The event was so nauseating that every time I recall it, the smell of rotting flesh comes back to me.

I guess the point is, we all need to reflect on past experiences and express ourselves. Otherwise, the traumas we suffer become the very weights that pull us down.

I do not regret my decision to stand up for what was right, no matter the consequences that laid in front of me. I embrace them and look forward to the revelry that comes with justice and truth. Who am I if not this?

It is common to repeat trauma. You can make progress while still holding on to the pain, because you are discovering new issues while overcoming others. That feeling of nothing working isn't positive, because you can judge yourself too harshly. You won't truly see the progress being made. Instead, you need to learn to express yourself and find your voice. In doing so, you will find people listening who care about you and your situation, who will be able to help you express your feelings to those you call family and friends.

As a child, it's hard to express when you've been the victim of a crime.

As a child, it's hard to express when you've been the victim of a crime, even if you are articulate. Society today requires definitive proof, and that unfortunately allows many rapists and criminals to go free.

When I followed the lives of those who hurt me, it became clear their antisocial behavior stemmed from self-importance. They lured their young prey using the radio waves, telling stories as children tried to sleep, trying to control what they see using hypnotic suggestion. They tried to create a bond, letting children sleep, then one of them dressed in black would creep into the children's rooms. The youngsters would think these perpetrators were there to save them from the monster these criminals had themselves created.

What parent believes their child when he or she says there's a monster under the bed?

Of course the criminals would ultimately poison the parent, try to immobilize them to rape the wife, attempt to humiliate and coerce the female into other acts, then extort the husband for payment.

To be clear, these atrocities happened to me between the ages of 3 and 8. When you look back as far as you can, what was your life like? What hopes and dreams did you have? What was stolen from you? I was about to learn the horrible truth.

After many years trapped in a cocoon of my own mind, I was thrust into a world I didn't know or remember. It was a world of celebrities, status, and wealth—a world I had actually helped build. It was extraordinary to me, like a Disney fairytale where a young prince comes to reclaim his kingdom. It was as if my mind was being opened to me for the first time since I was 8 years old. I had helped many there and was so loved and adored that it broke my heart.

I was so eager and ready to believe every word I heard. But I had to confront the darkness that laid before me, like a vast bottomless chasm of uncertainty and hopelessness—the how and the why it had all happened if I was so loved.

Why had they abandoned me in my darkest hour? It was like reaching over the hillside of luscious green grass only to be confronted by dark lands that needed to be crossed to reach the heavenly kingdom, where peace of mind and hope awaited.

Each of our lives is a story. The hero's journey is as old as time itself. It's easy to fall prey to doubts and fears, struggles we think we have overcome but that still lurk in a corner of the mind. What should cause joy quickly turns to pain and misery, a sadness as we gaze out a window upon the others seemingly without a care in the world. You might wonder, "Did I used to be that person? How can I become like that again?" Perhaps even, "Will I ever heal?" or "Will this journey ever truly be over?" Does anyone ever really get a happier ever after?

> *Why had they abandoned me in my darkest hour?*

With every trauma suffered it is hard to describe the feeling of helplessness, of loss, the pain that eats away at us because it cannot be undone. It is as everlasting as we are and can affect those we leave behind. I wonder are my loved ones safe? Are they happy? When will I see them again? Do they know I miss them? Am I a good man? Was I a good father? These questions never leave my mind.

Even as I write, having lost my home and children, desperately trying to find them again, I wonder about the intentions of others currently in my life. Are they here to help me? They may know me but they are hesitant to speak openly.

Every day more memories return. I want to take back what was rightfully mine so I can help my family, my friends, and the world to heal. In that healing, I want to show what can be achieved in just one life. Nothing is impossible.

You are the author of your own story, no matter how far you journey down that rabbit hole of life adventures. There are always better companions who can steer you to better shores and who have your back no matter the odds.

In truth then, remember that a thousand griefs can be shattered by a single joy, and while it is easy to dwell on what should have been, remember nothing worth doing is easy. You don't have to give up on any goal, because your dream can become reality at any age or after any trauma.

Good always conquers evil. So take a leap of faith, find a friend to lean on, never give up your light for another's, and remember that your journey's greatest moments are yet to happen.

DEVAN LIAM FEATHERSTONE

DEVAN LIAM FEATHERSTONE is a son, brother, cousin, friend, and super genius savant who once held the world in his hand. He did not stand on top and look down on others. Instead he tried every day to protect the things he loves and to elevate both himself and us so humanity could fulfil its true potential.

facebook.com/devan.featherstone

instagram.com/be._boldbe._brave

instagram.com/8ekind.today

Conclusion

Deana Brown Mitchell

After waking up in the hospital back in 1997, I did not know anything about suicide. Nor did I know there was help or resources available. I was not even familiar with a hotline, therapy, or organizations that focused on mental health.

For 23 years, I never once came across anything or anyone that made me feel like it was acceptable to discuss what I hid from the world for so long. I guess I assumed these things existed, but not for someone like me… I was a driven high achiever, a business owner, an executive, an employer.

The thought never crossed my mind that it was okay to talk about my depression. And I am not sure I even had words to explain it. When I was in that place, I just wanted to be alone. Talking about it would absolutely make me emotional, and in turn make me feel weak.

Then it happened in 2018… a friend of 20 years died by suicide. The news hit me like a ton of bricks.

What if he had known my story? Would he have talked to me? Would he still be here? I could never let this happen again… everything changed. Not sure what to do with this new outlook, it consumed my thoughts for months. I suddenly felt like I was on a mission to save everyone, and I did not care who knew.

But I was not ready to talk about my own story. Heck, I did not even remember details. After hiding so much for so long, I had to relive and process it all, which took time.

Conclusion ♦

There were three specific things that shaped my journey:

1. Music – specifically the song "Scars" by I Am They. This song helped me understand that the scars from my life were gifts that equipped me for what I believed was God's true purpose for my life on earth. I listened to this song thousands of times... sometimes on repeat for hours.

2. On January 4, 2020, I watched Shawn Johnson, Senior Pastor of Red Rocks Church, stand on stage in front of tens of thousands of people and share his personal journey of severe anxiety. I cried and cried and cried... then the revelation came. If he could stand up there and tell that story, I could too! *(It still took me a while.)*

3. On January 28, 2020, I turned 50. My husband took me to a tattoo parlor in Glenwood Springs, CO, and I proceeded to have my new mission permanently written on my forearm. I needed this constant reminder of what had transpired and my commitment to change the world of suicide ideation.

I could no longer hide from my past. I had to face it head on. Knowing that my commitment was to help others, I knew I would be unstoppable. I am one of the most determined and driven people you will ever meet. Call it my coping mechanism. *Scars to Stars*™ is the beginning of this vision coming to life.

No disrespect to anyone or to any organization that is working to prevent suicide, but the statistics have been rising every year for decades. What we are doing is not enough. It is *not working*.

Yes, we need a hotline. Yes, we need therapists. Yes, we need resources for people to pick and choose what helps them personally...

My theory is that we also need *hard conversations, community support*, and *personal raw stories* that people can relate to in their time of need.

Scars to Stars™ is about us meeting you in the midst of your pain to let you know you are not alone. We can relate to your struggle, and we care. People that have weathered similar storms can share how they made it through, giving you a helping hand in your own journey.

The revelation is that we *realize none of us are alone.* Everyone's journey is unique, but we can all help each other through our experiences. The connection that comes from this is invaluable.

The first time I met another suicide survivor, I no longer felt alone.

YOU ARE NOT ALONE.

YOU ARE WORTHY.

YOU ARE ENOUGH.

DEANA BROWN MITCHELL

DEANA BROWN MITCHELL is a driven, optimistic, and compassionate leader in all areas of her life.

As a bestselling author, speaker and award-winning entrepreneur, Deana vulnerably shares her experiences for the benefit of others. As a consultant/coach, she has a unique perspective on customizing a path forward for any situation.

Currently President of Genius & Sanity, she teaches her proprietary framework created from her own experiences of burnout and always putting herself last... for entrepreneurs and leaders who want to continue or expand their business while taking better care of themselves and achieving the life of their dreams.

In 2022 Deana released the book, *The Shower Genius: How Self-Care, Creativity & Sanity will Change Your Life Personally & Professionally*.

Also, Deana is the Founder and Executive Director of The Realize Foundation. She is a suicide survivor herself, and vulnerably uses her own mental health journey to let others know there is hope. The Realize Foundation produces events and publishes books that let people know they are not alone.

"But I will restore you to health and heal your wounds."
—Jeremiah 30:17

www.deanabrownmitchell.com

www.genius-and-sanity.com

www.realizefoundation.org

FIND OUT MORE

- **Scars to Stars™**
    - Buy the Book, Gift the Book, Donate the Book
        - Amazon, Barnes & Noble Website, Walmart Website
    - **Join the Scars to Stars LIVE Facebook Group**
        - https://www.facebook.com/groups/scarstostarslive
    - **Listen to the Scars to Stars Podcast**
        - https://feeds.captivate.fm/scars-to-stars-podcast/
    - **Visit our YouTube channel**
        - https://www.youtube.com/@realizefoundation5598

- **The Realize Foundation** https://realizefoundation.org/
    - Learn more about our **mission**
    - Take the FREE **H.O.P.E. Course**
    - **DONATE** to our cause
    - **Tell Your Story** (application on website, Scars to Stars page, QR Code Below)

- **Announcing our brand-new MEMBERSHIP!**
    - Learn more by scanning the QR Code Below

Membership   Tell Your Story

Made in the USA
Las Vegas, NV
13 September 2023

77514546R00121